EDWARD MACDOWELL
A Study

Da Capo Press Music Reprint Series

GENERAL EDITOR: FREDERICK FREEDMAN

Vassar College

EDWARD MACDOWELL
A Study

By Lawrence Gilman

New Introduction by Margery L. Morgan
American Symphony Orchestra League

𝄞 DA CAPO PRESS · NEW YORK · 1969

A Da Capo Press Reprint Edition

Library of Congress Catalog Number 67-27455

INTRODUCTION

ON May 8, 1900, twenty-one-year-old Lawrence
Gilman wrote to the well-known American composer, Edward MacDowell, requesting a copy
of MacDowell's lecture, "Suggestion in Music,"
delivered some months previously at Yale University. Gilman was then preparing an article on
MacDowell and his music. MacDowell drafted a
brief reply on May 12 apologizing for "being
unable to comply with your request. My notes
for the Yale lecture you allude to only represent
a part of my ideas on the subject and would
therefore be inadequate." Gilman went ahead,
nevertheless, and wrote his article. On August 1,
he sent a copy of it and a separate letter to Mac-
Dowell at Columbia University. By that time,
however, MacDowell was at his summer home in
Peterborough, New Hampshire, and Columbia
was forwarding only letters. The composer, therefore, had not yet been able to read Gilman's
article in the August 1 *Musical Record* ("Edward
MacDowell: An Appreciation") when he wrote

to thank Gilman—rather formally—for it on August 5. On the same day, he also drafted a letter to his friend, the Boston music critic, Philip Hale (who happened to be the editor of the *Musical Record*). "A man named Gilman has just written me that an article by him on my things has appeared in the Record—I presume it must be in part complimentary as *he* sent word to me about it. . . . If the thing is a scorcher, I depend upon you for the tip so I can skip it when we return to town."

A few days later, the *Musical Record* article reached MacDowell, having been forwarded from New York after all. Gilman's essay both pleased and amused him. On August 11, he wrote to Hale again—this time a much different kind of letter:

> Stupendous progressions—sumptuous purple-hued chords—luxuriant chromatics!!! Good Lord be kind to me a fool! Makes me feel as were I drunk with the blood of martyrs—I don't mean from a plagiaristic standpoint, but merely—well, well, "marvel of poetic imagery" "compelling fascination" "opulent in inspiration" "superb virility" "amazing fertility" etc. etc. etc., all this makes me dizzy—I say Hale, what a thunderingly mediocre cuss I must be to get all this praise—and yet I am fool enough to always get a thrill when people write to me they like my

music—But I will shut up on this—It was
good of you.—And I will write again when
I've gotten over the "portentous harmonies"
"masterly power" "superlatively lovely" "af-
fluent melodial beauty" "aglow with luminous
significance" "superb predominance" etc. etc.
etc. etc.

Holy smoke! Hale—

MacDowell then drafted a somewhat less formal
and more relaxed second "thank you" note to
Gilman.*

This was the first time Gilman had written an
article about MacDowell and it was not to be his
last. His association with MacDowell would cul-
minate with the publication of his *Edward Mac-
Dowell: A Study,* but his interest in MacDowell
and his music would endure long after Mac-
Dowell's death in 1908.

Lawrence Gilman was born in Flushing, New
York, in 1878. When his father died in 1893, he
went to Hartford to live with his paternal grand-
parents and there attended the Collins Street
Classical School. Two years later, he decided to
study art rather than go to college and returned
to New York to enroll in the Art Students'
League. Between 1896 and 1898, he worked as a
staff illustrator on the *New York Herald.* During

Infra, p. 60.

that time, he also developed an interest in music and taught himself theory, composition, piano, and organ. This interest soon became all-important, and he began a precarious career writing about music—his situation at the time of the *Musical Record* piece on MacDowell. In 1901, Gilman was appointed music critic of *Harper's Weekly;* subsequently, he served as the magazine's assistant editor (1903–1911) and managing editor (1911–1913). In 1913, he joined the editorial staff of *Harper's Magazine.* Two years later, he moved to the *North American Review* as music, drama, and literary critic, a position he held for eight years. He began to write program notes for the New York Philharmonic and the Philadelphia Orchestra in 1921, and from 1923 until his death in 1939, he was music critic of the *New York Herald Tribune.*

Throughout his career, Gilman constantly championed MacDowell and his music in books and articles, often writing in magazines other than those for which he regularly worked. He tried to keep MacDowell's name constantly before the public and devoted much time and energy to the MacDowell Club of New York City, established in October, 1905, when it became known that MacDowell was seriously ill.

In spite of the fact that numerous books and

hundreds of articles about MacDowell and his music were published after the appearance of Gilman's biography, *Edward MacDowell: A Study* (John Lane, 1908) still remains a major source of information about the man and his music. Gilman preceded the study with a monograph entitled *Edward MacDowell* (also published by Lane) in 1905. This eighty-page book contained very little about the composer's life and personal traits, a weakness which reviewers were quick to point out. In the 1908 study—the book was actually registered for copyright on December 31, 1908, although the title-page is dated 1909—Gilman tried to remedy its defects. He enlarged the biographical portion with the intention of presenting "a comprehensive, but not fully detailed, sketch" of MacDowell's career. He considered the revised version "a study, critical and speculative, rather than a formal life" of MacDowell. Among others, MacDowell's widow, Marian, assisted Gilman by furnishing detailed information, making copious suggestions, and reading proof. As a result, the biographical material and the factual data pertaining to the musical compositions are, with minor exceptions, extremely reliable. Therein lies the major worth of the book. Even with its flaws— among them, old-fashioned phrases and out-dated opinions, as well as a lack of documentation, bibliography, and index—the study remains the best of the MacDowell biographies, far superior in quality to Natalie Alden Putnam's *Edward MacDowell, Reminiscences and Romance* (1919) and Abbie Farwell Brown's factually correct but myth-making and prissy *The Boyhood of Edward MacDowell* (1924).

From a biographical standpoint, Gilman's study should be supplemented by a number of books and articles written subsequently by people who knew MacDowell personally. The most reliable of these (in chronological order) are: Mary Mears, "The Work and Home of Edward Mac-Dowell, Musician," *The Craftsman* (July, 1909); Henry F. Gilbert, "Personal Recollections of Edward MacDowell," *New Music Review* (November, 1912); T. P. Currier, "Edward MacDowell as I Knew Him," *The Musical Quarterly* (January, 1915); Templeton Strong, "Edward Mac-Dowell as I Knew Him," a twelve-article series in *The Music Student* (August, 1915, through July, 1916); William H. Humiston, *MacDowell* (1921); Leonard B. McWhood, "Edward Mac-Dowell at Columbia University," *Papers and Proceedings of the Music Teachers' National Association,* Eighteenth Series (1924); Upton Sinclair,

"Memories of Edward MacDowell," *Sackbut*
(December, 1925; also, *American Mercury,* Janu-
ary, 1926) ; Hamlin Garland, *Roadside Meetings*
(1930) and *Companions on the Trail* (1931) ;
John W. Burgess, *Reminiscences of an American
Scholar* (1934) ; and four John Erskine items:
"Edward Alexander MacDowell," in *Dictionary
of American Biography* (1937) ; "MacDowell at
Columbia: Some Recollections," *The Musical
Quarterly* (October, 1942) ; *The Memory of Cer-
tain Persons* (1947) ; and *My Life in Music*
(1950).

Since Erskine's reminiscences, only two significant contributions to the MacDowell literature
have appeared: the program for MacDowell's
installation into the New York University Hall
of Fame on October 25, 1964, and an article by
Irving Lowens, "Edward MacDowell," in *HiFi/
Stereo Review* (December, 1967).

The second half of Gilman's study, subtitled
"The Music-Maker," suffers not only from purple
prose and verbosity, but also from too many over-
enthusiastic critical judgments about MacDowell's
music. True, Gilman was aware of the danger of
following such a course. He pointed out in his
Preface that "posterity has an inconvenient habit

of reversing the judgments delivered upon creative artists by their contemporaries." He insisted that his evaluations of the music had "been set down with deliberation," but there is still too much Gilman and not enough MacDowell.*

Until the publication of the 1905 monograph, Gilman kept changing his mind about which works by MacDowell he preferred, and for many years, he and music critic Henry T. Finck, to whom the 1908 book is dedicated, pleasantly disagreed in print over their favorites. Nevertheless, the 1908 section about MacDowell's music remains far superior to Mrs. Crosby Adams' *What the Piano Writings of Edward MacDowell Mean to the Piano Student* (1913) and to John F. Porte's *Edward MacDowell* (1922). Somewhat better commentary can be found in G. C. Ashton Jonson's twenty-article series in *The Music Student* (April, 1911, through March, 1913), and in Percy A. Scholes' "MacDowell's Piano Works," also in *The Music Student* (August, 1915). The best work, however, came from Oscar G. Sonneck: "MacDowell *versus*

---

*MacDowell's musical thought is best revealed in his own words as compiled in the posthumous *Critical and Historical Essays,* brought out in 1912 by his friend and publisher, Arthur P. Schmidt. See reprint edition, New York, Da Capo Press, 1969.

MacDowell," an article which first appeared in
the *Papers and Proceedings of the Music Teach-
ers' National Association,* Sixth Series (1912)
and was later reprinted in Sonneck's *Suum cuique*
(1916) ; and the virtually definitive *Catalogue of
First Editions of Edward MacDowell* (1917).
Only four other items are reliable and important:
Humiston's "The Work of Edward MacDowell,"
*Papers and Proceedings of the Music Teachers'
National Association,* Third Series (1909) ; the
catalogue of the MacDowell exhibition held at
Columbia University in 1938; the *Supplement to
Sonneck's MacDowell Catalogue* (1942) prepared
by Richard S. Angell and issued by the Columbia
University Library (1942) ; and Marian Mac-
Dowell's *Random Notes on Edward MacDowell
and His Music* (1950).

While Gilman's 1908 study became an immediate favorite with many music lovers, it was not
greeted with joy everywhere. Youthfully enthusiastic and intensely partisan, Gilman made one
ill-chosen statement in regard to other contemporary American composers (page 173) which
caused controversy and inevitably harmed Mac-
Dowell's memory. An entry in an unpublished
diary kept by Templeton Strong, the composer's
close friend, describes his view of the situation
in 1934 :

I have just reread Lawrence Gilman's life of MacDowell which is excellent in many ways, very partisan as it should be and very sweeping in its appreciation of other American composers, as it should *not* be. Let me state at the outset of this note that my great admiration for MacDowell's talent and my affection for his memory remain unabated even though Gilman, in particular, in his life of MacDowell, and the MacDowell faction in general seem to have done their very best to render all the American composers inimical to MacDowell, not through praise of him, but through the sweeping condemnation of the work of his peers.

Gilman was justified in bestowing unstinted praise for MacDowell's rich talent, but his statement that all the other American composers are nullities whose works are negligible, was unjust, prejudiced, *invalidating* in a great measure his eulogies of MacDowell. Many American composers such as Chadwick, Kelley and others, had qualities of the highest order which MacDowell did not possess *at all* and which he regretted not possessing.

Now Gilman's manuscript . . . was undoubtedly submitted for approval and criticism to MacDowell's nearest adherents and *they allowed the amazing and wounding statement apropos of the other American composers to stand, thereby tacitly expressing their approbation and agreement.* This . . . did great harm to MacDowell's *cause* and to his mem-

> ory. . . . It was not necessary or wise to
> magnify MacDowell by belittling his peers
> and the effects of it not only remain but
> have rendered a vast portion of the musical
> public unduly critical of MacDowell's output.*

And so, in spite of MacDowell's unrivaled pop-
ularity during his lifetime and Gilman's well-
meant efforts, early indiscriminate praise and
subsequent changes in musical fashion have had
an adverse effect on MacDowell's posthumous
reputation. It is to be hoped that the old wounds
have now healed and that a more objective eval-
uation of MacDowell's worth as a composer will
allow him the important place he deserves in the
history of American music. Until that time comes,
however, Gilman's book gives us our deepest
insight into the life and work of an enigmatic
individual and unusually talented artist.

MARGERY L. MORGAN

American Symphony Orchestra League
Symphony Hill
Vienna, Virginia
November, 1967

---

*Passages from the Templeton Strong diary are cited
with the permission of Strong's literary executor, Georges
Perret of Geneva, Switzerland.

EDWARD MAC DOWELL

Edward MacDowell.

EDWARD MACDOWELL

A STUDY

By LAWRENCE GILMAN

AUTHOR OF

"*Phases of Modern Music*"; "*The Music of To-morrow*"; "*Stories of Symphonic Music*"; "*A Guide to Strauss' 'Salome'*"; "*Debussy's 'Pelléas et Mélisande': A Guide to the Opera*"; "*Aspects of Modern Opera*"; etc.

NEW YORK: JOHN LANE COMPANY
LONDON: JOHN LANE, THE BODLEY HEAD
MCMIX

The Plimpton Press Norwood Mass. U.S A.

PREFACE

THIS study is based upon the monograph on MacDowell which I contributed in 1905 to the "Living Masters of Music" series. That book could not, of course, remain in the series after the death of MacDowell three years later; it was therefore taken from its place and used as a foundation for the present volume, which supersedes it in every respect. The biographical portion is almost wholly new, and has been greatly enlarged, while the chapters dealing with Mac-Dowell's music have been revised and extended.

In completing this survey of one who in his art is still of to-day, I have been poignantly conscious throughout of the fact that posterity has an inconvenient habit of reversing the judgments delivered upon creative artists by their contemporaries; yet to trim deftly one's convictions in the hope that they may elastically conform to any one of a number of possible verdicts to be expected from a capricious futurity, is probably as dangerous a proceeding as to avow, without equivocation or compromise, one's precise beliefs.

It will therefore be understood that the critical estimates which are offered in the following pages have been set down with deliberation.

I desire to acknowledge gratefully the assistance which I have received from various sources: Primarily, from Mrs. Edward MacDowell, who has rendered help of an indispensable kind; from Mr. Henry T. Finck, who furnished me with his views and recollections of MacDowell as a pianist; and from reminiscences and impressions contributed by Mr. W. H. Humiston, Miss J. S. Watson, and Mr. T. P. Currier — pupils and friends of MacDowell — to *The Musician,* and by Mr. William Armstrong to *The Étude,* parts of which I have been privileged to quote. Mac-Dowell wrote surprisingly few letters, and comparatively little of his correspondence is of intrinsic or general interest. I am indebted to Mr. N. J. Corey for permission to quote from several in his possession; while for the use of letters written to MacDowell and his wife by Liszt and Grieg my thanks are due to Mrs. MacDowell.

L. G.

Dixville Notch, New Hampshire,
      September 18, 1908.

CONTENTS

ILLUSTRATIONS

. . . we grow immortal,
And that . . . harp awakens of itself
To cry aloud to the grey birds; and dreams,
That have had dreams for fathers, live in us.

— *The Shadowy Waters.*

THE MAN

MacDowell at Fourteen

(*From a Sketch drawn by Himself*)

THE MAN

CHAPTER I

RECORDS AND EVENTS

EDWARD MACDOWELL, the first Celtic voice that has spoken commandingly out of musical art, achieved that priority through natural if not inevitable processes. Both his grandfather and grandmother on his father's side were born in Ireland, of Irish-Scotch parents. To his paternal great-grandfather, Alexander MacDowell, the composer traced the Scottish element in his blood; his paternal great-grandmother, whose maiden name was Ann McMurran, was born near Belfast, Ireland. Their son, Alexander, born in Belfast, came to America early in the last century and settled in New York, where he married a countrywoman, Sarah Thompson, whom he met after his arrival in the New World. A son, Thomas (Edward's father), was born to them in New York — where, until his retirement some time ago, he was engaged in business for many years. He married in 1856 Frances M. Knapp, a young American woman of English antecedents. Five years later, on December 18,

1861, their third son, Edward Alexander (he discarded the middle name toward the end of his life), was born at 220 Clinton Street, New York — a neighbourhood which has since suffered the deterioration common to many of what were once among the town's most irreproachable residential districts.

From his father, a man of genuine æsthetic instincts, Edward derived his artistic tendencies and his Celtic sensitiveness of temperament, together with the pictorial instinct which was later to compete with his musical ability for decisive recognition; for the elder MacDowell displayed in his youth a facility as painter and draughtsman which his parents, who were Quakers of a devout and sufficiently uncompromising order, discouraged in no uncertain terms. The exercise of his own gift being thus restrained, Thomas Mac-Dowell passed it on to his younger son — a somewhat superfluous endowment, in view of the fact that the latter was to demonstrate so ample a gift for an equally effective medium of expression.

Edward had his first piano lessons, when he was about eight years old, from a friend of the family, Mr. Juan Buitrago, a native of Bogota, Colombia, and an accomplished musician. Mr. Buitrago was greatly interested in the boy, and had asked to be permitted to teach him his notes. Their piano practice at this time was subject to frequent interruptions; for when strict supervision was not exercised over his work, Edward was prone to indulge at the keyboard a fondness for composition which had developed concurrently with, and somewhat at the expense of, his proficiency in piano technique. He was not a prodigy, nor was he in the least precocious, though his gifts were as evident as they were various. He was not fond of drudgery at the keyboard, and he lacked the miraculous aptness at acquirement which belongs to the true prodigy. He was unusual chiefly by reason of the versatility of his gifts. His juvenile exercises in composition were varied by an apt use of the pencil and the sketching board. He liked to cover his music books and his exercises with drawings that showed both the observing eye and the naturally skilful hand of the born artist. Nor did music and drawing form a sufficient outlet for his impulse toward expression. He scribbled a good deal in prose and verse, and was fond of devising fairy tales, which were written not without a hint of the imaginative faculty which seems always to have been his possession.

He continued his lessons with Mr. Buitrago for several years, when he was taken to a professional piano teacher, Paul Desvernine, with whom he studied until he was fifteen. He received, too, at this time, occasional supplementary lessons from the brilliant Venezuelan, Teresa Carreño. When he was in his fifteenth year it was determined that he should go abroad for a course in piano and theory at the Paris Conservatory, and in April, 1876, accompanied by his mother, he left America for France. He passed the competitive examination for admission to the Conservatory, and began the Autumn term as a pupil of Marmontel in piano and of Savard in theory and composition — having for a fellow pupil, by the way, that most remarkable of contemporary music-makers, Claude Debussy, whom MacDowell described as having been, even then, a youth of erratic and non-conformist tendencies.

MacDowell's experiences at the Conservatory were not unmixed with perplexities and embarrassment. His knowledge of French was far from secure, and he had considerable difficulty in following Savard's lectures. It was decided, therefore, that he should have a course of tuition in the language. A teacher was engaged, and Edward began a resolute attack upon the linguistic *chevaux de frise* which had proved so troublesome an impediment — a move which brought him, unexpectedly enough, to an important crisis in his affairs.

On one occasion it happened that, during these lessons in French, he was varying the monotony of a study hour by drawing, under cover of his lesson-book, a portrait of his teacher, whose most striking physical characteristic was a nose of extravagant bulk. He was detected just as he was completing the sketch, and was asked, much to his confusion, to exhibit the result. It appears to have been a remarkable piece of work as well as an excellent likeness, for the subject of it was eager to know whether or not MacDowell had studied drawing, and, if not, how he acquired his proficiency. Moreover, he insisted on keeping the sketch. Not long after, he called upon Mrs. MacDowell and told her, to her astonishment, that he had shown the sketch to a certain very eminent painter — an instructor at the École de Beaux Arts — and that the painter had been so much impressed by the talent which it evidenced that he begged to propose to Mrs. MacDowell that she submit her son to him for a three-years' course of free instruction under his personal supervision, offering also to be responsible for his support during that time. The issue was a momentous one, and Mrs. MacDowell, in much perplexity of mind as to the wisest settlement of her son's future, laid the matter before Marmontel, who, fearful of losing one of his aptest pupils, urgently advised her against diverting her son from a musical career. The decision was finally left to MacDowell, and it was agreed that he should continue his studies at the Conservatory. Although it seems not unlikely that, with his natural facility as a painter and draughtsman and his uncommon faculties of vision and imagination, he would have achieved distinction as a painter, it may be questioned whether in that case music would not have lost appreciably more than art would have gained.

Conditions at the Conservatory were not to the taste of MacDowell, for he found his notions of right artistic procedure frequently opposed to those that prevailed among his teachers and fellow students. His growing disaffection was brought to a head during the summer of 1878. It was the year of the Exposition, and MacDowell and his mother attended a festival concert at which Nicholas Rubinstein played in memorable style Tchaikovsky's B-flat minor piano concerto. His performance was a revelation to the young American. "I never can learn to play like that if I stay here," he said resolutely to his mother, as they left the concert hall. Mrs. MacDowell, whose fixed principle it was to permit her son to decide his affairs according to his lights, thereupon considered with him the merits of various European Conservatories of reputation. They thought of Moscow, because of Nicholas Rubinstein's connection with the Conservatory there. Leipsic suggested itself; Frankfort was strongly recommended, and Stuttgart seemed to offer conspicuous advantages. The latter place was finally determined upon, and Mrs. MacDowell and her son went there from Paris at Thanksgiving time, having agreed that the famous Stuttgart Conservatory would yield the desired sort of instruction.

The choice was scarcely a happy one. It did not take MacDowell long to realise that, if he expected to conform to the Stuttgart requirements, he would be compelled to unlearn all that he had already acquired — would have virtually, so far as his technique was concerned, to begin *de novo*. Rubinstein himself, MacDowell was told by one of the students, would have had to reform his pianistic manners if he had placed himself under the guidance of the Stuttgart pedagogues. Nor does the system of instruction then in effect at the Conservatory appear to have been thorough even within its own sphere. MacDowell used to tell of a student who could play an ascending scale superlatively well, but who

was helpless before the problem of playing the
same scale in its descending form.

His mother, disheartened over the failure of
Stuttgart to justify her expectations, was at a loss
how best to solve the problem of her son's immediate future. Having heard much of the ability
of Carl Heymann, the pianist, as an instructor,
Mrs. MacDowell thought of the Frankfort Conservatory, of which Joachim Raff was the head,
and where Heymann would be available as a
teacher.

She learned from a friend, to whom she had
written for advice, that the pianist had promised
soon to visit her at her home in Wiesbaden, and
it was suggested that the MacDowells pay her a
visit at the same time, and thus benefit by the
opportunity of becoming acquainted with Heymann. Mrs. MacDowell and her son were not
slow to avail themselves of this proposal, and the
end of the year 1878 found them in Wiesbaden.
Here they met Heymann, who had just concluded
a triumphantly successful *tournée* of the European
capitals. They heard him play, and were impressed by his mastery and poetic feeling. Heymann was not, however, to begin teaching at the
Frankfort Conservatory until the following autumn, so MacDowell remained in Wiesbaden,
studying composition and theory with the distin-

MacDowell at eighteen (the figure at the extreme left of the group) as a member of Raff's class at the Frankfort Conservatory

It looks like him though not well

drawn

A SKETCH OF LISZT BY MacDOWELL DRAWN IN 1883

guished critic and teacher, Louis Ehlert, while
his mother returned to America.

"Ehlert," MacDowell has written, "was very
kind to me, and when I asked him for 'lessons' he
refused flatly, but said he would be glad for us
to 'study together,' as he put it. This rather
staggered me, as my idea in leaving Paris was to
get a severe and regenerating overhauling. I
worked hard all winter, however, and heard lots
of new music at the *Cur Haus*, which was like
manna in the desert after my long French famine.
Ehlert, who thought that Heymann was not the
man for me, spoke and wrote to Von Bülow about
me; but the latter, without even having seen me,
wrote Ehlert a most insulting letter, asking how
Ehlert dared 'to propose such a silly thing' to
him; that he was not a music teacher, and could
not waste his time on an American boy, anyway.
So, after all, I went to Frankfort and entered the
conservatory." MacDowell's first interview with
Raff, in the autumn of 1879, was, as he relates,
"not promising." "Heymann took me to him
and told him, among other things, that, having
studied for several years the 'French School' of
composition, I wished to study in Germany.
Raff immediately flared up and declared that
there was no such thing nowadays as 'schools'
— that music was eclectic nowadays; that if some

French writers wrote flimsy music it arose simply from flimsy attainments, and such stuff could never form a 'school.' German and other writers were to be criticised from the same standpoint — their music was bad, middling, or good; but there was no such thing as cramping it into 'schools' nowadays, when all national musical traits were common property."

MacDowell remained in the Conservatory for two years, studying composition with Raff and piano with Heymann. His stay there was eminently satisfactory and profitable to himself. He found both Raff and Heymann artistic mentors of an inspiring kind; in Raff, particularly, he encountered a most sympathetic and encouraging preceptor, and an influence at once potent and engrossing — a force which was to direct the currents of his own temperament into definite artistic channels.

For Heymann as a pianist MacDowell had a fervent admiration. He spoke of him as "a marvel," whose technique "seemed mysteriously capable of anything." "When I went to him," MacDowell has said, "I had already transposed most of the fugues and preludes of Bach (Paris ideas of 'thoroughness'!) and had gone through much rough technical work. Heymann let me do what I wanted; but in hearing him practise

and play I learned more in a week than I ever
had before." When Heymann, who had already
begun to show symptoms of the mental disorder
which ultimately overcame him, left the Conservatory in 1881, he recommended MacDowell
as his successor — a proposal which was cordially
seconded by Raff. But there were antagonistic
influences at work within the Conservatory.
MacDowell's candidacy was opposed by certain
of the professors, on account, it was said, of his
"youth"; but also, doubtless, because of the
advocacy of Heymann, who was not popular
with his colleagues; for he dared, MacDowell
has said, "to play the classics as if they had
been written by men with blood in their veins."
So MacDowell failed to get the appointment.
He continued, unofficially, as a pupil of Heymann, and went to him constantly for criticism
and advice.

MacDowell began at this time to take private
pupils, and one of these pupils, an American, Miss
Marian Nevins, was later to become his wife.
He was then living in lodgings kept by a venerable
German spinster who was the daughter of one of
Napoleon's officers. She was very fond of her
young lodger, and through her he became acquainted with the work of Erckmann-Chartrian,
whose tales deeply engrossed him at this time.

Later he moved to the Café Milani, on the Zeil, at that time an institution of considerable celebrity. As a teacher he made a rather prominent place for himself; the recommendation of Raff — who had said to one of MacDowell's pupils that he expected "great things" of him — had helped at the start, and his personality counted for not a little. His appearance at this time (he was then nineteen years old) is described as having been strikingly unlike that of the typical American as known in Germany. "His keen and very blue eyes, his pink and white skin, reddish mustache and imperial and jet black hair, brushed straight up in the prevalent German fashion, caused him to be known as 'the handsome American.'" Teaching at that time must have been a sore trial to him. He was, as he continued to be throughout his life, painfully shy; yet he seems, strangely enough, to have had, even then, the knack for imparting instruction, for quickening the interest and stimulating the enthusiasm of those who came under his guidance, which in later years made him so remarkable a teacher.

In 1881 MacDowell applied for the vacant position of head piano teacher at the Conservatory in the neighbouring town of Darmstadt, and was engaged. He found it an arduous and not too profitable post. He has described it as "a dreary town, where the pupils studied music with true German placidity." They procured all their music from a circulating library, where the choice of novelties was limited to late editions of the classics and a good deal of sheer trash, poor dance music and the like. His work, which was unmitigated drudgery, consumed forty hours a week. For a time he took up his quarters in Darmstadt; but he missed the attractions of Frankfort; so throughout his term he travelled on the railroad twice daily between the two towns. In addition to his regular work at the Conservatory, he undertook private lessons, going by train once a week to the Erbach-Fürstenau castle at Erbach-Fürstenau, a wearisome three-hour journey. The castle was a mediæval *Schloss*, with a drawbridge and moat. There his pupils were little counts and countesses, discouragingly dull and sleepy children who spoke only German and Latin, and who had the smallest interest in music. MacDowell gave them lessons in harmony as well as piano-playing, and one day, in the middle of an elaborately simplified exposition of some rudimentary point, he heard a gentle noise, looked around from the piano, and discovered his noble young pupils with their heads on their arms, fast asleep. MacDowell could never remember their different titles, and ended by addressing them simply as "mademoiselle" and "monsieur," to the annoyance of the stern and ceremonious old châtelaine, the Baroness of Rodenberg.

The twelve hours a week which he spent in railway travelling were not, though, wholly unprofitable, for he was able to compose on the train the greater part of his second "Modern Suite" for piano (op. 14). This was the second of his compositions which he considered worthy of preservation, its predecessor being the "First Modern Suite," written the year before in Frankfort.   Much other music had already found its way upon paper, had been tried in the unsparing fire of his criticism, which was even then vigorous and searching, and had been marked for destruction — a symphony, among other efforts. His reading at this time was of engrossing interest to him.   He was absorbed in the German poets; Goethe and Heine, whom he was now able to read with ease in the original German, he knew by heart — a devotion which was to find expression a few years later in his "Idyls" and "Poems" (op. 28 and 31).   He had begun also to read the English poets.   He devoured Byron and Shelley; and in Tennyson's "Idyls of the King" he found the spark which kindled his especial love for mediæval lore and poetry. Yet while he was enamored of the imaginative records of the Middle Ages, he had little interest, oddly enough, in their tangible remains. He liked, for example, to summon a vision of the valley of the Rhone, with its slow-moving human streams flowing between Italy and the North, and with Sion still looking down from its heights, where the bishops had been lords rather than priests. But this was for him a purely imaginative enchantment. He cared little about exploring the actual and visible memorials of the past: to confront them as crumbling ruins gave him no pleasure, and, as he used to say, he "hated the smells." It was this instinct which, in his visits to the cathedrals, prompted him to stand as far back as possible while the Mass was being said. To see in the dim distance the white, pontifical figures moving gravely through the ritual, to hear the low tones, enthralled and stirred him; but he shrank from entering the sacristy, with its loud-voiced priests describing perfunctorily the relics: that was a disillusionment not to be borne with.

Having found that his labours at Darmstadt were telling upon his health, MacDowell resigned his position there and returned to Frankfort. Here he divided his time between his private teaching and his composition. He was ambitious also to secure some profitable concert engagements as a pianist. He had made occasional appearances at orchestral concerts in Wiesbaden, Frankfort, Darmstadt, but these had yielded him no return save an increase of reputation.

At Raff's instigation he visited Liszt at Weimar in the spring of 1882, armed with his first piano concerto (op. 15). This work he had just composed under amusing circumstances. One day while he was sitting aimlessly before his piano there came a knock at his door, and in walked, to his startled confusion, his master, Raff, of whom MacDowell stood in unmitigated awe. "The honor," he relates, "simply overwhelmed me. He looked rather quizzically around at my untidy room, and said something about the English translation of his *Welt-Ende* oratorio (I found out after, alas, that he had wanted me to copy it in his score for him; but with his inexplicable shyness he only hinted at it, and I on my side was too utterly and idiotically overpowered to catch his meaning); then he abruptly asked me what I had been writing. I, scarcely realising what I was saying, stammered out that I had a concerto. He walked out on the landing and turned back, telling me to bring it to him the next Sunday. In desperation, not having the remotest idea how I was to accomplish such a task, I worked like a beaver, evolving the music from some ideas upon which I had planned at some time to base a concerto. Sunday came, and I had only the first movement composed. I wrote him a note making some wretched excuse, and he put it off until the Sunday after. Something happened then, and he put it off two days more; by that time I had the concerto ready." Except for three lines of passage work in the first part, the concerto remains to-day precisely as MacDowell finished it then.

In the event, the visit to Liszt, which he had dreaded, was a gratifying surprise. That beneficent but formidable personage received him with kindly courtesy, and had Eugen D'Albert, who was present, play the orchestral part of the concerto which MacDowell had brought with him in manuscript, arranged for two pianos. Liszt listened attentively as the two young musicians played it through, — not too effectively, — and when they had finished he commended it in warm terms. "You must bestir yourself," he warned D'Albert, "if you do not wish to be outdone by our young American"; and he praised the boldness and originality of certain passages in the music, especially their harmonic treatment.

What was at that time even more cheering to MacDowell, who had not yet come to regard him-

self as paramountly a composer, was Liszt's praise
of his piano playing. He returned to Frankfort
greatly encouraged, and he was still further
elated to receive soon after a letter from Liszt in
which, referring to the first "Modern Suite,"
which MacDowell had sent to him, the Abbé
wrote:

" . . . Since the foundation of the General Society of
German Musicians, the definitive making up of the pro-
grams is entrusted to me, and I shall be very glad to
recommend the execution of your work.

"Will you be good enough to give to your master, my
old friend, J. Raff, the assurance of my highest esteem
and admiration.

"F. LISZT.

"Budapest.   April 13, 1882."

The nineteenth annual convention of the *All-
gemeiner Deutscher Musik-Verein* was held that
year at Zürich, from the 9th to the 12th of July;
and at the fifth concert of the series, on July 11,
MacDowell played his first piano suite. Both
the music and his performance of it were
praised. A contemporaneous account speaks of
the composer as "an earnest and modest musician,
free from all mannerisms," who "carried his
modesty so far that he played with his notes
before him, though he cannot have felt any particular necessity for having them there." He

Monsieur,

Dans une huitaine de jours
je serai de retour à Weimar
et m'informerai aussitôt, auprès
de M. Riedel, du sort de
votre Suite moderne (en manuscrit)
Depuis la fondation de l'Allgemeine
deutsche Tonkünstler Verein, la rédaction
définitive des programmes m'est
communiquée; il me sera fort
agréable de recommander l'exécution
de votre ouvrage.
Veuillez redire à votre maître,
mon ancien ami J. Raff, mes constants
sentiments de haute estime admirative.
affectueusement
F. Liszt
13 avril. 82. Budapest.

FACSIMILE OF A LETTER FROM LISZT TO MACDOWELL
(SEE PAGE 18)

A LETTER FROM LISZT TO MACDOWELL ACCEPTING THE DEDICATION OF THE FIRST PIANO CONCERTO (SEE PAGE 19) "was recalled enthusiastically, and with many bravos, and may be proud of the success he has achieved." Until then, as MacDowell confessed, with engaging candour, to Mr. Henry T. Finck, he "had never waked up to the idea" that his music could be worth actual study or memorising. "I would not have changed a note in one of them for untold gold, and *inside* I had the greatest love for them; but the idea that any one else might take them seriously had never occurred to me." A year later, upon Liszt's recommendation, the suite and its successor, the "Second Modern Suite," op. 14, were published at Leipzig by the famous house of Breitkopf and Härtel. "Your two pianoforte suites," wrote Liszt from Budapest, in February of that year, "are admirable. I accept the dedication of your concerto with sincere pleasure and thanks." The suites were the first of MacDowell's works to appear in print.*

The death of Raff on June 25, 1882, brought to MacDowell his first profound sorrow. There was a deep attachment between pupil and master, and MacDowell felt in Raff's death the loss of a sincere friend, and, as he later came to appreciate, a powerful ally. The influential part which Raff

* The "Two Old Songs," which bear an earlier opus number, — 9, — were composed at a much later period — a fact which is betrayed by their style.

bore in turning MacDowell's aims definitely and permanently toward creative rather than pianistic activity could scarcely be overestimated. When he first went to Paris, and during the later years in Germany, there had been little serious thought on his part, or on the part of his family, concerning his composition; his evident talent for piano-playing had persistently overshadowed his creative gifts, and had made it seem that his inevitable career was that of a virtuoso. As he wrote in after years: "I had acquired from early boyhood the idea that it was expected of me to become a pianist, and every moment spent in 'scribbling' seemed to be stolen from the more legitimate work of piano practice." It was Raff — Raff, who said to him once: "Your music will be played when mine is forgotten" — who opened his eyes.

The two following years, —from the summer of 1882 till the summer of 1884 — were increasingly given over to composition, though MacDowell continued his private teaching and made a few appearances in concert. He continued to try his hand at orchestral writing, and in this pursuit he was greatly favoured by the willingness of the conductors of the *Cur-Orchesters* at Baden-Baden, Wiesbaden, and elsewhere, to "try over" in the rehearsal hour his experiments.

His requests for such a trial reading of his
scores were seldom refused, and the practical
training in instrumentation which was afforded
by the experience he always regarded as invalu-
able. Much that he tested in this manner was
condemned as a result of the illuminating, if
chastening, revelations thus brought about; and
almost all of his orchestral writing which he afterward thought fit to publish received the benefit
of such practical tests.

The music which dates from this period comprises the three songs of opus 11 ("*Mein Lieb-
chen*," * "*Du liebst mich nicht*," "*Oben, wo die
Sterne glühen*"); the two songs of op. 12 ("*Nacht-
lied*" and "*Das Rosenband*"); the Prelude and
Fugue (op. 13); the second piano suite (op. 14)
— begun in the days of his Darmstadt professorship; the "Serenade" (op. 16); the two "*Fantasiestücke*" of op. 17: "*Erzählung*" and the
much-played "*Hexentanz*"; the "*Barcarolle*"
and "*Humoreske*" of op. 18; and the "*Wald-
Idyllen*" (op. 19): "*Waldesstille*," "*Spiel der
Nymphen*," "*Träumerei*," "*Dryadentanz*."

In June, 1884, MacDowell returned to America,
and on July 21, at Waterford, Connecticut, he
was married to his former pupil, Miss Marian

* I give the German titles under which these compositions
were originally published.

Nevins — a union, which, for perfection of sympathy and closeness of comradeship, was, during the quarter of a century for which it was to endure, nothing less than ideal. A few days later MacDowell and his bride sailed from New York for Europe, innocent of any very definite plans for the immediate future. They visited Exeter and Bath, and then went to London, where they found lodgings at No. 5, Woburn Place. There MacDowell's interest in the outer world was divided between the British Museum, where he found a particular fascination in the Egyptian and Syrian antiquities, and the Shakespearian performances of Henry Irving and Ellen Terry. He was captivated by their performance of "Much Ado About Nothing," and made a sketch for a symphonic poem which was to be called "Beatrice and Benedick" — a plan which he finally abandoned. Most of the material which was to form the symphonic poem went ultimately to the making of the scherzo of the second piano concerto, composed during the following year.

Returning to Frankfort, MacDowell and his wife lived for a short time in a pension in the Praunheimer Strasse, keeping very much to themselves in two small rooms. Upon their return from a brief excursion to Paris, they found less restricted quarters in the Hotel du Nord. In

September of this year MacDowell learned of an advantageous position that had been vacated at the Würzburg Conservatory, and, assisted by letters from Frau Raff, Marmontel (his former instructor at the Paris Conservatory), and the violinist Sauret, he sought the place. But again, as at Frankfort three years before, his youth was in his disfavour, and he was courteously rejected.

The following winter was given over largely to composition. The two-part symphonic poem, "Hamlet and Ophelia," his first production of important significance, was composed at this time. The "*Drei Poesien*" (op. 20) and "*Mondbilder*" (op. 21), both written for four-hand performance, also date from the winter of 1884–85, and the second piano concerto was begun. The "Moon Pictures" of op. 21 ("The Hindoo Maiden," "Stork's Story," "In Tyrol," "The Swan," "Visit of the Bear"), after Hans Christian Andersen, were at first intended to form a miniature orchestral suite; but an opportunity arose to have them printed as piano duets, and the orchestral sketches were destroyed — a regrettable outcome, as it seems.

His pupils, he found, were scattered, and he gave himself up without restraint to the pleasures of creative writing. These were days of quiet and deep happiness. He read much, often aloud

in the evening — fairy-tales, of which he was
devotedly fond, legendary lore of different coun-
tries, mediæval romances, Keats, Shelley, Tennyson, Benvenuto Cellini's Memoirs, Victor Hugo,
Heine; and also Mark Twain. Later, in the
spring, the days were devoted partly to composition and partly to long walks with his wife
in the beautiful Frankfort woods, where was
suggested to MacDowell the particular mood
that found embodiment, many years later, in
one of the last things that he wrote: "From a
German Forest," in the collection of "Fireside
Tales."

The following summer (1885), the death of a
friend of his earlier Frankfort days, Lindsay
Deas, a Scotchman, left vacant in Edinburgh the
post of examiner for the Royal Academy of
Music, and Deas's family presented MacDowell's
name as a candidate. A trip to London was
undertaken for the purpose of securing the place,
if possible — since composition alone could not
be depended upon for a livelihood; but again his
youth, as well as his nationality and his "modern
tendencies," militated against him. He was
obliged to admit that he had been a protégé of
"that dreadful man Liszt," as the potentate of
Weimar was characterised by Lady Macfarren,
an all-powerful factor in the control of the insti-

tution; and that proving finally his abandonment to a nefarious modernity, he was again rejected.

Upon their return to Germany the MacDowells moved from Frankfort to Wiesbaden, where they spent the winter of 1885–86, living in a small pension. The first concerto (op. 15) had recently been published by Breitkopf and Härtel. The same year (1885) was marked by the completion of the second concerto in D-minor, begun at Frankfort in the previous winter, and the publication by Breitkopf and Härtel of the full score of "Hamlet and Ophelia,"* with a dedication to Henry Irving and Ellen Terry, from whose performances in London MacDowell had caught the suggestion for the music. In the summer of 1886 MacDowell and his wife again yielded to their passion for travelling and went to London to buy furniture, for they had wearied of living in pensions and hotels and had determined to set

* The published score of this opus bears the title (in German): "Hamlet; Ophelia: Two Poems for Grand Orchestra." But MacDowell afterward changed his mind concerning this designation, and preferred to entitle the work: "First Symphonic Poem (a. 'Hamlet'; b. 'Ophelia')." This alteration is written in MacDowell's handwriting in his copy of the printed score. When "Lancelot and Elaine" was published three years later it bore the sub-title: "Second Symphonic Poem."

up housekeeping. When they returned they hired a little flat in the Jahnstrasse and installed themselves there with just enough furniture to give them countenance. Here Mrs. MacDowell suffered an illness which threatened for a time to bring a tragic termination to their happiness, and through which the hope of a child was lost to them.

One afternoon in the spring of 1887 MacDowell and his friend Templeton Strong, a brilliant American composer who had recently moved from his home in Leipzig to Wiesbaden, were tramping through the country when they came upon a dilapidated cottage on the edge of the woods, in the Grubweg. It had been built by a rich German, not as a habitation, but as a kind of elaborate summer house. The situation was enticing. The little building stood on the side of the Neroberg, overlooking the town on one side, with the Rhine and the Main beyond, and on the other side the woods. The two Americans were captivated by it, and nothing would do but that MacDowell should purchase it for a home. There was some question of its practicability by his cooler-headed wife; but eventually the cottage was bought, with half an acre of ground, and the MacDowells ensconced themselves. There was a small garden, in which MacDowell delighted to dig;

the woods were within a stone's throw; and he and Strong, who were inseparable friends, walked together and disputed amicably concerning principles and methods of music-making, and the need for patriotism, in which Strong was conceived to be deficient.

This was a time of rich productiveness for MacDowell; and the life that he and his wife were able to live was of an ideal serenity and detachment. He was now devoting his entire energy to composition. He put forth during these years at Wiesbaden the four pieces of op. 24 ("Humoresque," "March," "Cradle Song," "Czardas"); the symphonic poem "Lancelot and Elaine" (op. 25); the six songs, "From An Old Garden," to words by Margaret Deland (op. 26); the three songs for male chorus of op. 27 ("In the Starry Sky Above Us," "Springtime," "The Fisherboy"); the "Idyls" and "Poems" for piano (op. 28 and op. 31), after Goethe and Heine; the symphonic poem "Lamia" (op. 29); the two "Fragments" for orchestra after the "Song of Roland": "The Saracens" and "The Lovely Aldâ" (op. 30); the "Four Little Poems" for piano — "The Eagle," "The Brook," "Moonshine," "Winter" (op. 32); the three songs of op. 33 ("Prayer," "Cradle Hymn," "Idyl") and the two of op. 34 ("Menie," "My Jean");

and the "Romance" for 'cello and orchestra.[*]
He had, moreover, the satisfaction of knowing
that his work was being received, both in Europe
and in his own country, with interest and respect.
His reputation had begun unmistakably to spread.
"Hamlet and Ophelia" had been performed at
Darmstadt, Wiesbaden, Baden-Baden, Sonders-
hausen, Frankfort. On March 8, 1884, his former
teacher, Teresa Carreño, had played his second
piano suite at a recital in New York; in March
of the following year two movements from the
first suite were played at an "American Concert"
given at Princes' Hall, London; on March 30,
1885, at one of Mr. Frank Van der Stucken's
"Novelty Concerts" in New York, Miss Adele
Margulies played the second and third movements from the first piano concerto. In the
same year Mme. Carreño played on tour in
America three movements from the second suite,
and in the following September she played at
the Worcester Festival of that year the "*Hexentanz*" of op. 17. On November 4, 1886, the
"Ophelia" section of op. 22 was performed at
the first of Mr. Van der Stucken's "Symphonic Concerts" at Chickering Hall, New
York. Mr. H. E. Krehbiel, reviewing the work
in the *Tribune*, praised the orchestration as
"brilliant" ("though the models studied are

*Op. 35. Another work, the "Etude de Concert" (op. 36),
was completed in Wiesbaden. [Ed.]

rather more obvious than we like"), the melodic invention as "beautiful" and as having a poetical mood and characteristic outline. He considered that the music deserved repetition during the course of the season, and pronounced it "a finer work in every respect than the majority of the novelties which have come to us this season with French and English labels." Mr. Henry T. Finck, writing in the *Evening Post*, characterised the work as "an exquisitely conceived tone-poem, charmingly orchestrated and full of striking harmonic progressions." A year after the performance of the "Ophelia" in New York Mr. Van der Stucken produced its companion piece, "Hamlet." In April, 1888, at the first of a course of "pianoforte-concerto concerts" given by Mr. B. J. Lang at Chickering Hall, Boston, MacDowell's first concerto was played by Mr. B. L. Whelpley. "The effect upon all present," wrote Mr. W. F. Apthorp in the *Transcript*, "was simply electric." The concerto "was a surprise, if ever there was one. We can hardly," he declared, "recall a composition so full of astonishing and unprecedented effects [it will be recalled that this concerto was composed in 1882, when MacDowell was twenty years old]. The work was evidently written at white heat; its brilliancy and vigour are astounding. The impression it made

upon us, in other respects, is as yet rather un-
digested . . . But its fire and forcibleness are
unmistakable." These opinions are of interest,
for they testify to the prompt and ungrudging
recognition which was accorded to MacDowell's
work, from the first, by responsible critics in his
own country.

He might well have felt some pride in the sum
of his achievements at this time. He had not
completed his twenty-seventh year; yet he had
published a concerto and two orchestral works of
important dimensions—"Hamlet and Ophelia"
and "Lancelot and Elaine"; most of the music
that he had so far written had been publicly
performed, and almost invariably praised with
warmth; and he was becoming known in Europe
and at home. His material affairs, however,
were far from being in a satisfactory or promising condition; for there was little more than a
precarious income to be counted upon from his
compositions; and he had given up teaching.
Musicians from America began coming to the
little Wiesbaden retreat to visit the composer
and his wife, and he was repeatedly urged to
return to America and assume his share in the
development of the musical art of his country.
It was finally decided that, all things considered,
conditions would be more favorable in the United

States; and in September, 1888, the MacDowells sold their Wiesbaden cottage, not without
many pangs, and sailed for their own shores.

They settled in Boston, as being less huge and
tumultuous than New York, and took lodgings
in Mount Vernon Street. In later years they
lived successively at 13 West Cedar Street and
at 38 Chestnut Street. Though all of his more
important music was as yet unwritten, Mac-
Dowell found himself already established in the
view of the musical public as a composer abundantly worthy of honour at the hands of his coun-
trymen. He made his first public appearance in
America, in the double capacity of pianist and
composer, at a Kneisel Quartet concert in Chickering Hall, Boston, on November 19, 1888, playing
the Prelude, Intermezzo, and Presto from his
first piano suite, and, with Kneisel and his asso-
ciates, the piano part in Goldmark's B-flat Quin-
tet. He was cordially received, and Mr. Apthorp,
writing in the *Transcript* of his piano playing,
praised his technique as "ample and brilliant,"
and as being especially admirable "in the higher
phases of playing"; "he plays," wrote this critic,
"with admirable truth of sentiment and musical
understanding." Of the early and immature
suite he could not well write with much enthusiasm, though he found in it "life and brightness."

In the following spring MacDowell made a more auspicious appearance, and one which more justly disclosed his abilities as a composer, when, on March 5, he played his second concerto, for the first time in public, at an orchestral concert in Chickering Hall, New York, under the direction of Mr. Theodore Thomas. His success was then immediate and emphatic. Mr. Krehbiel, in the *Tribune*, praised the concerto as "a splendid composition, so full of poetry, so full of vigor, as to tempt the assertion that it must be placed at the head of all works of its kind produced by either a native or adopted citizen of America"; and he confessed to having "derived keener pleasure from the work of the young American than from the experienced and famous Russian" — Tchaikovsky, whose Fifth Symphony was performed then for the first time in New York. "Several enthusiastic and unquestionably sincere recalls," concluded the writer, "were the tokens of gratitude and delight with which his townspeople rewarded him." A month later Mac-Dowell played the same concerto in Boston, at a Symphony concert, under Mr. Gericke; his performance of it evoked "rapt attention," and "the very heartiest of plaudits, in which both orchestra and audience joined."

In the summer of that year (1889) MacDowell

and his wife went abroad. He had been invited to take part in an "American Concert" at the Paris Exposition, and on July 12, under Mr. Van der Stucken's direction, he played his second concerto.* After a short stay on the continent, he returned with his wife to America.

MacDowell found in Boston a considerable field for his activity as pianist and teacher. He took many private pupils, and he made, during the eight years that he remained there, many public appearances in concert. In composition, these years were the most fruitful of his life. He wrote during this period the Concert Study for piano (op. 36);†the set of pieces after Victor Hugo's "*Les Orientales*" (op. 37) — "*Clair de lune*," "*Dans le Hamac*," "*Danse Andalouse*"; the "Marionettes" (op. 38); the "Twelve Studies" of op. 39; the "Six Love Songs" (op. 40); the two songs for male chorus (op. 41) — "Cradle Song" and "Dance of the Gnomes"; the orches-

* The rest of the programme, it may be interesting to note, contained Arthur Foote's overture, "In the Mountains," Van der Stucken's suite, "The Tempest," Chadwick's "Melpomene" overture, Paine's "Œdipus Tyrannus" prelude, a romance and polonaise for violin and orchestra by Henry Holden Huss, and songs by Margaret Ruthven Lang, Dudley Buck, Chadwick, Foote, Van der Stucken. The concert ended with an "*ouverture festivale sur l'Hymne Américaine*, ' The Star Spangled Banner,' " by Dudley Buck.

†But see p. 28 fn. [Ed.]

tral suite in A-minor (op. 42) and its supplement,
"In October" (op. 42–A);* the "Two Northern
Songs" and "Barcarolle" (op. 43 and op. 44)
for mixed voices; the "Sonata Tragica" (op. 45);
the 12 "Virtuoso Studies" of op. 46; the "Eight
Songs" (op. 47); the second ("Indian") suite for
orchestra; the "Air" and "Rigaudon" (op. 49)
for piano; the "Sonata Eroica" (op. 50); and the
"Woodland Sketches" (op. 51). This output
did not contain his most mature and characteristic works — those were to come later, during
the last six years of his creative activity; yet
the product was in many ways a notable one,
and some of it — the two sonatas, the "Indian"
suite, the songs of op. 47, the "Woodland
Sketches" — was, if not consistently of his very
best, markedly fine and characteristic in quality.
This decade (from 1887 to 1897) saw also the
publication of all his work contained between
his op. 22 ("Hamlet and Ophelia") and op. 51
(the "Woodland Sketches") with the exception
of the symphonic poem "Lamia," which was
not published until after his death.

* This episode formed part of the suite in its original form,
but was not printed until several years after the publication
of the rest of the music. The earlier portion, comprising
four parts ("In a Haunted Forest," "Summer Idyll," "The
Shepherdess' Song," "Forest Spirits"), was published in
1891, the supplement in 1893.

Meanwhile his prestige grew steadily. Each new work that he put forth met with a remarkable measure of success, both among the general public and at the hands of many not over-complacent critical appraisers. On January 10, 1890, his "Lancelot and Elaine" was played at a Boston Symphony concert under Mr. Nikisch. In September, 1891, his orchestral suite in A-minor (op. 42) was performed for the first time at the Worcester Festival, and a month later it was played in Boston at a Symphony concert under Mr. Nikisch. In November of the same year the Boston Philharmonic Orchestra, under Bernhard Listemann, performed for the first time, at the Tremont Theatre, his "Roland" pieces, "The Saracens" and "The Lovely Aldâ." On the following day — November 6, 1891 — he gave his first piano recital, playing, in addition to pieces by Bach, Schubert, Schumann, Templeton Strong, P. Geisler, Alabieff, and Liszt, his own "Witches' Dance," "Shadow Dance" (op. 39), "The Eagle," the Étude in F-sharp (op. 36), the Prelude from the first suite, and the fourth of the "Idyls" after Goethe. He followed this with a second recital in January, 1892, at which he played, among other things, the "Winter," "Moonshine," and "The Brook," from the "Four Little Poems" (op. 32). Discussing the first of these recitals, Mr. Philip Hale (in the *Boston Post*) wrote these words, which have a larger application than their reference to Mac-Dowell: "No doubt, as a composer, he has studied and mastered form and knows its value; but he prefers suggestions and hints and dream pictures and sleep-chasings to all attempts to be original in an approved and conventional fashion. . . . They [his compositions] are interesting, and more than that: they are extremely characteristic in harmonic colouring. Their size has nothing to do with their merits. A few lines by Gautier stuffed with prismatic words and yet as vague as mist-wreaths may in artistic worth surpass whole cantos of more famous poets; and Mr. Mac-Dowell has Gautier's sense of colour and knowledge of the power of suggestion." His performance "was worthy of the warmest praise . . . seeing gorgeous or delicate colours and hearing the voices of orchestral instruments, it is no wonder that Mr. MacDowell is a pianist of rare fascina-tion." On January 28, 1893, the "Hamlet and Ophelia" was played, for the first time in Boston, by the Symphony Orchestra under Mr. Nikisch; but a more important event was the first performance* two months later of the

* A single movement of the "Sonata Tragica," the third, was played by MacDowell in Boston on March 18, 1892, at

"Sonata Tragica," which MacDowell played at a Kneisel Quartet concert in Chickering Hall. Concerning the sonata Mr. Apthorp wrote: "One feels genius in it throughout — and we are perfectly aware that *genius* is not a term to be used lightly. The composer," he added, "played it superbly, magnificently." MacDowell achieved one of the conspicuous triumphs of his career on December 14, 1894, when he played his second concerto with the Philharmonic Society of New York, under the direction of Anton Seidl. He won on this occasion, recorded Mr. Finck in the *Evening Post*, "a success, both as pianist and composer, such as no American musician has ever won before a metropolitan concert audience. A Philharmonic audience can be cold when it does not like a piece or a player; but Mr. MacDowell . . . had an ovation such as is accorded only to a popular prima donna at the opera. Again and again he had to get up and bow after every movement of his concerto; again and again was he recalled at the close. . . . For once a prophet has had great honour in his own country. . . . He played with that splendid kind of virtuosity which makes one forget the technique." Concerning the concerto, Mr. W. J. Henderson wrote (in the

the last of the three recitals which he gave in that season at Chickering Hall.

Times) that it was difficult to speak of it "in terms of judicial calmness, for it is made of the stuff that calls for enthusiasm. There need be no hesitation," he continued, "in saying that Mr. MacDowell in this work fairly claims the position of an American master. We may have no distinctive school of music, but here is one young man who has placed himself on a level with the men owned by the world. This D-minor concerto is a strong, wholesome, beautiful work of art, vital with imagination, and made with masterly skill." And Mr. James Huneker observed that "it easily ranks with any modern work in this form. Dramatic in feeling, moulded largely, and its themes musically eloquent, it sounds a model of its kind — the kind which Johannes Brahms gave the world over thirty years ago in his D-minor concerto." In March of the following year MacDowell gave two piano recitals in the Madison Square Garden Concert Hall, New York, playing, beside a number of his smaller pieces, his "Tragica" sonata, which made, if anything, an even profounder impression than it had made in Boston two years before. Probably the most signal of the honours that came to him at this time was paid him when the Boston Symphony Orchestra placed both his "Indian" suite and his first concerto on the programme of its New York

concert on January 23, 1896, at the Metropolitan
Opera House.

In the spring of 1896 it was determined to
found a department of music at Columbia University, New York. This was made possible
by a fund of $150,000 given to the trustees
by Mrs. Elizabeth Mary Ludlow, with the pro-
viso that the income was to be applied in such
ways as should "tend more effectually to elevate
the standard of musical instruction in the United
States, and to afford the most favourable opportunity for acquiring musical instruction of the
highest order." In May of that year the professorship was offered to MacDowell, the com-
mittee who had the appointment in charge
announcing the consensus of their opinion to
be that he was "the greatest musical genius
America has produced." MacDowell, though
he valued greatly the honour of his selection,
considered anxiously the advisability of accepting
the post. He now had more pupils than he could
take, and his pecuniary circumstances would not
be improved by the change, save that a settled
income would be assured to him. This was of
course a tempting prospect; on the other hand,
the task of organizing *de novo* a new department
in a large university, and the curtailed freedom
which the position would necessitate, made him

hesitate. But the assurance of an income free from precariousness finally decided him in favour of acceptance; and in the following autumn he moved from Boston to New York, and began his duties at Columbia.

That he undertook his labours there, from the start, in no casual or perfunctory spirit, is made clear by the bare record of his activity. For the first two years of his incumbency he had no assistant, carrying all the work of his department on his own shoulders. He devoted from eight to ten hours a week to lectures and class-work; and this represented but a small proportion of the time and labour expended in establishing the new department. The aim of the instruction was to be twofold. "First, to teach music scientifically and technically, with a view to training musicians who shall be competent to teach and to compose. Second, to treat music historically and æsthetically as an element of liberal culture." This plan involved five courses of study, and a brief description of them will indicate the scope of the task undertaken by MacDowell.

There was to be, first, a "general musical course," consisting of lectures and private reading, with illustrations. This course, while "outlining the purely technical side of music," aimed at giving "a general idea of music from its historical and æsthetic side," and it treated of "the beginnings of music, the Greek modes and their evolution, systems of notation, the Troubadours and Minnesingers, counterpoint and fugue, beginnings of opera, the clavecinists, beginnings of programme music, harmony, beginnings of the modern orchestra, evolution of forms, the symphony and opera up to Beethoven." A second course (this was not begun until the following year) treated "of the development of forms, the song, romanticism, instrumental development, and the composers for pianoforte, revolutionary influences, the virtuoso, modern orchestration and symphonic forms, the music-drama, impressionism versus absolute music, color *versus* form, the relationship of music to the other arts, musical criticism." A third course treated of "general theory, dictation, harmony, comprising chords and their mutual significance, altered chords, suspensions, modulation, imitation, analysis, and the commencement of composition in the smaller forms." A fourth course comprised, in the first term, counterpoint, canon, choral figuration, and fugue; in the second term, "free counterpoint, canon and fugue, analysis, commencement of composition in the larger forms." The fifth course treated of "free composition, analysis, instrumentation, symphonic forms," and the study of "all the orchestral and other instruments, considered collectively and individually," together with demonstrations of their "technique, possibilities, and limitations."

At the end of the second year an assistant was appointed —a gentleman who had been a student in the department.   To him were entrusted the classes in rudimentary harmony, dictation, and chord-analysis; and to this extent he relieved MacDowell until the latter had his sabbatical vacation in 1902–03; he then took over the classes in strict counterpoint; but all the more advanced courses were discontinued until MacDowell's return.   Even with an assistant, however, MacDowell found his labours very far from being light.   In his third year (1898–99) he still gave five courses of two hours a week each, with the exception of a single one-hour course.   For these no less than eighty-six students were registered; and in the following year, fifty-two students were registered in one of the courses. In 1901–02 he gave six courses: a general course in musical culture, for which he had thirty-seven students; an advanced course in musical culture, for which he had fourteen students; a course in counterpoint, twelve students; in orchestration, twelve students; in practical composition, thirteen students; in free compositions, two students.

This continued to be, in general, his work until he resigned in 1904. To these labours he added the appalling drudgery of correcting examination books and exercises — a task which he performed with unflagging patience and invariable thoroughness. Some of his friends remember seeing him at this particular labour, and they recall "the weary, tired, though interested face; the patient trying-over and annotating." In addition to his regular duties, he devoted every Sunday morning to receiving students in the more advanced courses who were invited to come to him for help in their composition and piano work. He was, as his friend Hamlin Garland has said, "temperate in all things but work — in that he was hopelessly prodigal."

These facts are worth stating in detail; for it has been said that MacDowell had no drudgery to perform at Columbia; that he had few students, and that the burden of the teaching work was borne by his assistant. The impression has gone abroad that he had little didactic capacity, that he was disinclined toward and disqualified for methodical work. It cannot, of course, be said that his inclinations tended irresistibly toward pedagogy, or that he loved routine. Yet that he had uncommon gifts as a teacher, that he was singularly methodical in his manner of work, are

facts that are beyond question. His students
have testified to the strikingly suggestive and
illuminating manner in which his instruction was
imparted. His lectures, which he wrote out in
full, are remarkable for the amount of sheer
"brain-stuff" that was expended upon them.
They are erudite, accurate, and scholarly; they
are original in thought, they are lucid and stimulating in their presentation and interpretation of
fact, and they are often admirable in expression.
They would reflect uncommon credit upon a
writer who had given his life to the critical, historical, and philosophical study of music; as
the work of a man who had been primarily absorbed in making music, rather than in discussing
it, they are extraordinary.

As conveying an idea of MacDowell's methods
in the class-room I cannot do better than quote
from a vivid account of him in this aspect
written by one of his pupils, Miss J. S. Watson:

"A crowd of noisy, expectant students sat in
the lecture room nervously eyeing the door and
the clock by turns. The final examination in
course I of the Department of Music was in progress in the back room, the door of which opened
at intervals as one pupil came out and another
went in. The examination was oral and private,

and when the door closed behind me Professor MacDowell, who was standing at the open window, turned with a smile and motioned me toward a chair.   In a pedagogic sense it was not a regular examination.   There was something beautifully human in the way the professor turned the traditional stiff and starched catechism into a delightfully informal chat, in which the faburden, the Netherland School, early notation, the great clavichord players, suites and sonatas, formed the main topics.   The questions were put in such an easy, charming way that I forgot to be frightened; forgot everything but the man who walked rapidly about the room with his hands in his pockets and his head tipped slightly to one side; who talked animatedly and looked intently at the floor; but the explanations and suggestions were meant for me.   When I tripped upon the beginning of notation for instruments, he looked up quickly and said, 'Better look that up again; that's important.'

"At the lectures Professor MacDowell's aim had been to emphasise those things that had served to mark the bright spots in the growth and advancement of music as an intelligible language. How well I recall my impression on the occasion of my first visit to the lectures, and afterwards! There was no evidence of an æsthetic side to the equipment of the lecture room. At the end it was vast and glaringly white, and except for an upright piano and a few chairs placed near the lecturer's table the room was empty. Ten or twelve undergraduates, youths of eighteen or twenty, and twenty or more special students and auditors, chiefly women, were gathered here. The first lectures, treating of the archaic beginnings of music, might have easily fallen into a business-like recital of dates, but Professor Mac-Dowell never sank into the passionless routine of lecture giving. His were not the pedantic discourses students link most often to university chairs. They were beautifully illuminating talks, delivered with so much freedom and such a rush of enthusiasm that one felt that the hour never held all that wanted to be said, and the abundant knowledge, in its longing to get out, kept spilling over into the to-morrows.

"His ideas were not tied up in a manuscript, nor doled out from notes. They came untrammelled from a wonderfully versatile mind, and were illustrated with countless musical quotations and interlined with a wealth of literary and historical references. There was no regular textbook; some students carried a Rockstro or a Hunt, but the majority depended upon the references made during the lectures. These were numerous, and gave a broad view of this speculative period in musical history.

"Music was brought from behind the centuries and spread before us like a huge map. Whatever meaning lay hidden under the musical theories of the ancients was explained in a clear and conscientious way. Short decisive sentences swept into every obscure corner, and from all sides we saw reflected Professor MacDowell's resolute spirit and sincerity of purpose. . . .

"To illustrate [a point in connection with a discussion of popular music], Professor Mac-Dowell went to the piano to play 'A Hot Time in the Old Town To-night.' After playing a few measures, he turned abruptly toward the class, saying: 'Why, that isn't it! What is it I am playing?' Someone answered 'Annie Rooney.' Facing us with a droll smile, he asked if there was anyone present who could play 'A Hot Time.' A dozen boys rushed forward and the one who gained the chair dashed it off with the abandon of a four weeks' old freshman . . .

"The lectures on musical form were distinguished by many brilliant demonstrations of MacDowell's genius. The ease and rapidity with which he flashed his thoughts upon the blackboard were both inspiring and bewildering to the student who must grope his way through notes before he can reach an idea. If any were unwise enough to stop even for a moment to catch these spontaneous thoughts as they flew along the staff, they were very apt upon looking up to see them vanishing like phantoms in a cloud of white chalk. At the same time he made sarabandes, gavottes, minuets, chaconnes, passepieds, gigues, polonaises and rondos dance across the piano in quick succession; and his comments were as spirited as his playing.

"Professor MacDowell's criticisms were clear and forceful, and filled with many surprising and humorous touches. Of Bach he said, 'Bach spoke in close, scientific, contrapuntal language. He was as emotional and romantic as Chopin, Wagner or Tchaikovsky; his emotion was expressed in the language of his time. Young women who say they adore Bach play him like a sum in mathematics. They find a grim pleasure in it, like biting on a sore tooth.'

"He never approached the piano like a conqueror. He had a nervous way of saying that he didn't know whether things would go, because he had had no time to practise. After an apologetic little preamble, he would sit down and play these rococo bits of trailing sound with fingers dipped in lightning, fingers that flashed over the keys in perfect evenness and with perfect sureness.

"The closing lectures were in reality delightfully informal concerts for which the class began to assemble as early as 8.30 in the morning. By 9.30 every student would be in his chair, which he had dragged as near to the piano as the early suburbanite would let him. Someone at the window would say, 'Here he comes!' and, entering the room with a huge bundle of music under one arm and his hat in his hand, MacDowell would deposit them on the piano and turn to us with his gracious smile. Then, instead of sitting down, he would continue to walk up and down the room, his thoughts following, apparently, the pace set by his energetic steps. He had an abundant word supply and his short, terse sentences were easy to follow."

This is not the picture of a man who was unqualified for his task, or indifferent, rebellious, or inept in its performance; it is the picture of a man of vital and electric temperament, with almost a genius — certainly with an extraordinary gift — for teaching. His ideals were lofty; he dreamed of a relationship between university instruction and a liberal public culture which was not to be realised in his time. He was anything but complacent; had he been less intolerant in his hatred of unintelligent and indolent thought on the subjects that were near his heart, his way would have been made far easier.

The results of his labours at the university, he finally came to feel, did not warrant the expenditure of the vitality and time that he was devoting to them. He was, in a sense, an anachronism in the position in which he found himself. Both in his ideals and in his plans for bringing about their fulfilment he had reached beyond his day. The field was not yet ripe for his best efforts. It became clear to him that he could not make his point of view operative in what he conceived as the need for a reformation of conditions affecting his work; and on January 18, 1904, after long and anxious deliberation and discussion with his wife, he tendered his resignation as head of the department. His attitude in the matter was grievously misunderstood and misrepresented at the time, to his poignant distress and harassment. The iron entered deeply into his soul: it was the forerunner of tragedy.

When he took up his work at Columbia his activity as a concert pianist had, of course, to be virtually suspended. With the exception of two short tours of a few weeks' each, he gave up his public appearances altogether until the year of his sabbatical vacation (1902–03). In December, 1902, he went on an extensive concert tour, which took him as far west as San Francisco and occupied all of that winter. The following spring and summer were spent abroad, in England and on the Continent. In London he appeared in concert, playing his second concerto with the Philharmonic Society on May 14. He returned to America in October, and resumed his work at Columbia.

Meanwhile his composition had continued uninterruptedly. Indeed, the eight years during which he held his Columbia professorship were, in a creative sense, the most important of his life; for to this period belong the "Sea Pieces" (op. 55), the two superb sonatas, the "Norse" (op. 57) and the "Keltic" (op. 59), and the best of his songs — the four of op. 56 ("Long Ago," "The Swan Bent Low to the Lily," "A Maid Sings Light," "As the Gloaming Shadows Creep"), and the three of op. 58 ("Constancy," "Sunrise," "Merry Maiden Spring"): a product which contains the finest flower of his inspiration, the quintessence of his art.* He wrote also during these years the three songs of op. 60 ("Tyrant Love," "Fair Springtide," "To the Golden Rod"); the "Fireside Tales" (op. 61); the "New England Idyls" (op. 62); numerous part-songs,

* The only one of his works of equal calibre which does not, strictly speaking, belong to this period is the set of "Woodland Sketches"; these were composed during the last part of his stay in Boston, and were published in the year (1896) of his removal to New York.

transcriptions, arrangements; and, finally, the greater part of a suite for string orchestra which he never finished to his satisfaction: in fact, nearly one quarter of the bulk of his entire work was composed during these eight years. During this period, moreover, was published all of the music hitherto unprinted which he cared to preserve.

He had bought in 1896 a piece of property near the town of Peterboro, in southern New Hampshire, consisting of a small farmhouse, some out-buildings, fifteen acres of arable land, and about fifty acres of forest. The buildings he consolidated and made over into a rambling and comfortable dwelling-house; and in this rural "*asyl*" (as Wagner would have called it), surrounded by the woods and hills that he loved, he spent his summers from then until the end of his life. There most of his later music was written, in a small log cabin which he built, in the heart of the woods, for use as a workshop. Thus his summers were devoted to composition, and his winters to the arduous though absorbing labours of his professorship; in addition, he taught in private a few classes for which he made time in that portion of the day which was not taken up by his sessions at the university. During his first two winters in New York he also

served as conductor of the Mendelssohn Glee
Club, and he was for a time president of the
Manuscript Society, an association of American
composers. Altogether, it was a scheme of
living which permitted him virtually no opportunity for the rest and idleness which he imperatively needed.

In New York the MacDowells' home was, during the first year, a house in 88th Street, near
Riverside Drive. Later they lived at the Majestic
Hotel; but during most of the Columbia years —
from 1898 till 1902 — they occupied an apartment
at 96th Street and Central Park West. After
their return from the sabbatical vacation abroad
they lived for a year at the Westminster Hotel in
Irving Place, and for a year in an apartment house
on upper Seventh Avenue, near Central Park.
When that was sold and torn down they returned
to the Westminster; and there MacDowell's last
days were spent.

After he left Columbia in 1904, he continued
his private piano classes (at some of which he
gave free tuition to poor students in whose talent
he had confidence). He should have rested —
should have ceased both his teaching and his
composing; for he was in a threatening condition.
Had he spent a year in a sanitarium, or had he
stopped all work completely and taken even a

brief vacation, he might have averted the collapse
which was to come. In the spring of 1905 he
began to manifest alarming signs of nervous
exhaustion. A summer in Peterboro brought no
improvement. That autumn his ailment was
seen to be far more deeply seated than had been
supposed. There were indications of an obscure
brain lesion, baffling but sinister. Then began a
very gradual, progressive, and infinitely pathetic
decline — the slow beginning of the end. He
suffered little pain, and until the last months he
preserved in an astonishing degree his physical
well-being. It was clear almost from the start
that he was beyond the aid of medical science,
even the boldest and most expert. A disinte-
gration of the brain-tissues had begun — an
affection to which specialists hesitated to give a
precise name, but which they recognized as
incurable. His mind became as that of a little
child. He sat quietly, day after day, in a chair
by a window, smiling patiently from time to
time at those about him, turning the pages of a
book of fairy tales that seemed to give him a
definite pleasure, and greeting with a fugitive
gleam of recognition certain of his more intimate
friends. Toward the last his physical condition
became burdensome, and he sank rapidly. At
nine o'clock on the evening of January 23, 1908,

in the beginning of his forty-seventh year, he died at the Westminster Hotel, New York, in the presence of the heroic woman who for almost a quarter of a century had been his devoted companion, counsellor, helpmate, and friend. After such simple services as would have pleased him, held at St. George's Episcopal Church, on January 25, his body was taken to Peterboro; and on the following day, a Sunday, he was buried in the sight of many of his neighbours, who had followed in procession, on foot, the passage of the body through the snow-covered lane from the village. His grave is on an open hill-top, commanding one of the spacious and beautiful views that he had loved. On a bronze tablet are these lines of his own, which he had devised as a motto for his "From a Log Cabin," the last music that he wrote:

"A house of dreams untold,
  It looks out over the whispering tree-tops
  And faces the setting sun."

CHAPTER II

In his personal intercourse with the world, MacDowell, like so many sensitive and gifted men, had the misfortune to give very often a wholly false account of himself. In reality a man of singularly lovable personality, and to his intimates a winning and delightful companion, he lacked utterly the social gift, that capacity for ready and tactful address which, even for men of gifts, is not without its uses. It was a deficiency (if a deficiency it is) which undoubtedly cost him much in a material sense. Had he possessed this serviceable and lubricant quality it would often have helpfully smoothed his path. For those who could penetrate behind the embarrassed and painful reticence that was for him both an impediment and an unconscious shield, he gave lavishly of the gifts of temperament and spirit which were his; even that lack of ready address, of social adaptability and adjustment, which it is possible to deplore in him, was, for those who knew him and valued him, a not

MacDowell and Templeton Strong
From a photograph taken at Wiesbaden in 1888

MacDowell in 1892

uncertain element of charm: for it was akin to
the shyness, the absence of assertiveness, the
entirely genuine modesty, which were of his
dominant traits. Yet in his contact with the
outer world this incurable shyness sometimes, as
I have said, led him into giving a grotesquely
untrue impression of himself: he was at times
gauche, blunt, awkwardly infelicitous in speech
or silence, when he would have wished, as he
knew perfectly how, to be considerate, gentle,
sympathetic, responsive. On the other hand,
his shyness and reticence were seemingly contra-
dicted by a downright bluntness, a deliberate
frankness in matters of opinion in which his
convictions were involved; for his views were
most positively held and his convictions were
often passionate in intensity, and he declared
them, upon occasion, with an utter absence of
diplomacy, compromise, or equivocation; with a
superb but sometimes calamitous disregard of
his own interests.

Confident and positive to a fault in his ad-
herence to and expression of his principles, he
was as morbidly dubious concerning his own
performances as he was uneasy under praise. He
was tortured by doubts of the value of each new
work that he completed, after the flush and
ardour generated in its actual expression had

passed; and he listened to open praise of it in evident discomfort. I have a memory of him on a certain occasion in a private house following a recital at which he had played, almost for the first time, his then newly finished "Keltic" Sonata. Standing in the center of a crowded room, surrounded by enthusiastically effusive strangers who were voluble — and not over-penetrating — in their expressions of appreciation, he presented a picture of unhappiness, of mingled helplessness and discomfort, which was almost pathetic in its genuineness of woe. I was standing near him, and during a momentary lull in the amiable siege of which he was the distressed object, he whispered tragically to me: "Can't we get out of this? — Do you know the way to the back door?" I said I did, and led him through an inconspicuous doorway into a comparatively deserted corridor behind the stair-case. I procured for him, through the strategic employment of a passing servant, something to eat, and we staid in concealment there until the function had come to an end, and his wife had begun to search for him. He was quite happy, consuming his salad and beer behind the stairs and telling me in detail his conception of certain of the figures of Celtic mythology which he had had in mind while composing his sonata.

To visitors at his house in Peterboro, he said one morning, on leaving them, "I am going to the cabin to write some of my rotten melodies!" He was sincerely distrustful concerning the worth of any composition which he had finished; especially so, of course, concerning his more youthful performances. He once sent a frantic telegram to Teresa Carreño, upon learning from an announcement that she was to play his early Concert Étude (op. 36) for the first time: "Don't put that dreadful thing on your programmè"; and for certain of his more popular and hackneyed pieces, as the "Hexentanz" and the much-mauled and over-sentimental song, "Thy Beaming Eyes," he had a detestation that was amusing in its virulence. He regretted at times that his earlier orchestral works — "Hamlet and Ophelia" and "Lancelot and Elaine" — had been published; and he was invariably tormented by questionings and misgivings after he had committed even his ripest work to his publisher. Only the assurances of his wise and devoted wife at times prevented him from recalling a completed work. Yet he was always touched, delighted, and genuinely cheered by what he felt to be sincere and thoughtful praise. To a writer who had published an admiring article concerning some of his later music he wrote:

"My dear Mr. ———:

Your article was forwarded to me after all. I wish to thank you for the warm-hearted and sympathetic enthusiasm which prompted your writing it. While my outgivings have always been sincere, I feel only too often their inadequacy to express my ideals; thus what you speak of as accomplishment I fear is often but attempt. Certainly your sympathy for my aims is most welcome and precious to me, and I thank you again most heartily."

Those who knew the man only through his music have thought of him as wholly a dreamer and a recluse, a poet brooding in detachment, and unfriendly to the pedestrian and homely things of the world. Nothing could be further from the truth. He was overflowingly human, notably full-blooded. On his "farm" (as he called it) at Peterboro he lived, when he was not composing, a robust and vigorous outdoor life. He was an ardent sportsman, and he spent much of his time in the woods and fields, fishing, riding, walking, hunting. He had a special relish for gardening and for photography, and he liked to undertake laborious jobs in carpentry, at which he was quite deft. That his feeling for the things of the natural world was acutely sensitive and coloured by imagination and emotion is abundantly evidenced in his music. He was fond of taking long, leisurely drives and rides

through the rich and varied hill country about
Peterboro, and many of the impressions that were
then garnered and stored have found issue in
some of his most intimate and affecting music —
as in the "Woodland Sketches" and "New England Idyls." He had an odd, naïve tenderness
for growing things and for the creatures of the
woods: it distressed him to have his wife water
some of the flowers in the garden without water-
ing them all; and though an excellent shot, he
never brought down game without a pang — it
used to be said at Peterboro that for this reason
he only "pretended to hunt," despite his expert-
ness as a marksman.

In his intellectual interests and equipment he
presented a striking contrast to the brainless-
ness of the average musician. His tastes were
singularly varied and catholic. An omnivorous
reader of poetry, an inquisitive delver in the
byways of mediæval literature, an authority in
mythological detail, he was at the same time
keenly interested in contemporary affairs. He
read, and discussed with eagerness and acumen,
scientific, economic, and historical deliverances;
and he enjoyed books of travel, biographies,
dramatic literature. Mark Twain he adored,
and delighted to quote, and almost to the end of
his life he read with inexhaustible pleasure Joel

Chandler Harris's "Uncle Remus." In the later
years of his activity he fell captive to the new
and unaccustomed music of Fiona Macleod's
exquisite prose and verse; he wanted to dedicate
his "New England Idyls" to the author of
"Pharais" and "From the Hills of Dream,"
and wrote for her permission; but the identity
of the mysterious author was then jealously
guarded, and his letter must have gone astray;
for it was never answered.

His erudition was extraordinary. He exemplified in a marked degree the truth that the
typical modern music-maker touches hands with
the whole body of culture and the humanities
in a sense which would have been simply incred-
ible to Mozart or Schubert. He was, intellec-
tually, one of the most fully and brilliantly
equipped composers in the history of musical art.
He had read widely and curiously in many lit-
eratures, and the knowledge which he had acquired he applied to the elucidation of æsthetic
and philosophical problems touching the theory
and practice of music. He had meditated deeply
concerning the art of which he was always a
tireless student — had come to conclusions concerning its actual and assumed records, its
tendencies, its potentialities. He was a vigorous and original critic, and he had shrewd,

cogent, and clear-cut reasons for the particular views at which he had arrived; whether one could always agree with them or not, they invariably commanded respect. Yet his erudition was seldom displayed. One came upon it unexpectedly in conversation with him, through the accident of some reference or the discussion of some disputed point of fact.

In his appearance MacDowell suggested a fusion of Scandinavian and American types. His eyes, of a light and brilliant blue, were perhaps his most salient feature. They betrayed his inextinguishable humour. When he was amused — and he was seldom, in conversation, grave for long — they lit up with an extraordinary animation; he had an unconscious trick of blinking them rapidly once or twice, with the effect of a fugitive twinkle, which was oddly infectious. His laugh, too, was communicative; he did not often laugh aloud; his enjoyment found vent in a low, rich chuckle, which, with the lighting up of his eyes, was wholly and immediately irresistible. The large head, the strong, rather boyish face, with its singular mobility and often sweetness of expression, the bright, vital eyes, set wide apart, the abundant (though not long), dark hair tinged with grey, the white skin, the sensitive mouth, rather large and full-lipped, the strong jaws, the sturdy and athletic build, — he was somewhat above medium height, with broad shoulders, powerful arms, and large, muscular, finely shaped hands, — his general air of physical soundness and vigour: all these combined to form an outer personality that was strongly attractive. His movements were quick and decisive. To strangers, even when he felt at ease, his manner was diffident, yet of an indescribable, almost childlike, simplicity and charm. His voice in speaking was low-pitched and subdued, like his laugh; in conversation, when he was entirely himself, he could be brilliantly effective and witty, and his mirth-loving propensities were irrepressible.

His sense of humour, which was of true Celtic richness, was fluent and inexhaustible. To an admirer who had affirmed in print that certain imaginative felicities in some of the verse which he wrote for his songs recalled at moments the phrasing of Whitman and Shakespeare, he wrote:

"I will confide in you that if, in the next world, I should happen upon the wraiths of Shakespeare, Whitman, and Co., I would light out without delay. Good heavens! I blush at the thought of it! A header through a cloud would be the only thing. — Seriously, I was deeply touched by your praise and wish I were more worthy."

His pupil and friend, Mr. W. H. Humiston,

recalls that, in going over MacDowell's sketch-books and manuscripts after his death, he found that many of the manuscripts had been rewritten several times: "I would find a movement begun and continued for half a page, then it would be broken off suddenly, and a remark like this written at the end: — 'Hand organ to the rescue!'"

I told him once that I had first heard his "To a Wild Rose" played by a high-school girl, on a high-school piano, at a high-school graduation festivity. "Well," he remarked, with his sudden illumination, "I suppose she pulled it up by the roots!" Some one sent him at about this time, relates Mr. Humiston, a programme of an organ recital which contained this same "Wild Rose" piece. "He was not pleased with the idea, having in mind the expressionless organ of a dozen years ago when only a small portion of most organs was enclosed in a swell-box. Doubt-less thinking also of a style of organ performance which plays Schumann's *Träumerei* on the great organ diapasons, he said it made him think of a hippopotamus wearing a clover leaf in his mouth."

A member of one of his classes at Columbia, finding some unoccupied space on the page of his book after finishing his exercise, filled up the space with rests, at the end of which he placed a double bar. When his book was returned the page was covered with corrections — all except these bars of rests, which were enclosed in a red line and marked: "This is the only correct passage in the exercise."

He once observed in a lecture that "Bach differed in almost everything from Handel, except that he was born the same year and was killed by the same doctor."

He was often sarcastic; but his was a sarcasm without sting or rancour. Bitterness, indeed, was one of the few normal attributes which he did not possess. Mr. Humiston tells of lunching with him unexpectedly at a restaurant one day, just after his resignation from Columbia had been accepted. "We sat over our coffee and cigars until nearly four o'clock, and among other things he talked of that [the Columbia matter]. There was not a word of bitterness or reproach toward anyone, but rather a deep feeling of disappointment that his plans and ideals for the training and welfare of young artists should have been so completely defeated."

In his methods of work he was, like most composers of first-rate quality, at the mercy of his inspiration. He never composed at the piano, in the ordinary meaning of the phrase. That is to say, he never sat down to the piano with the idea

that he wanted to compose a song or a piano piece.
But sometime, when he might be improvising, as
he was fond of doing when alone, a theme, an
idea, might come to him, and almost before he
knew it he had sketched something in a rudimentary form. He had a fancy that the technique of composition suffered as much as that of
the piano if it was allowed to go for weeks and
months without exercise. The constant work and
excitement that his winters in Boston and New
York involved, made it necessary for him to let
days and weeks slip by with no creative work
accomplished. Yet he always tried to write each
day a few bars of music. Often in this way he
evolved a theme for which he afterward found a
use. In looking over a sketch-book in the summer he would run across something he liked, and
the idea would expand into a matured work.

His sketch-books are full of all kinds of random
and fugitive material — half-finished fugues,
canons, piano pieces, songs, single themes. Undoubtedly this habit of work had its value when
he came to the leisurely months of summer;
for he did not then have to go through a period
of technical "warming up." There were many
days when he did not write a note, but he always
intended to, and usually did. When he was absorbed in a particular composition he kept at it,

almost night and day, save for the hours he always tried to spend in the open air, and two hours in the evening when, no matter how late it might be, he sat quietly with his wife, reading or talking, smoking, and, in earlier days, enjoying a glass of beer and some food. His love of reading was a godsend to him when the waters were more than usually troubled and his brain was in a whirl.

In the actual work of composition he was elaborately meticulous — not often to the extent of changing an original plan, but in minor details; he never ceased working on a score until the music was out of his hands, or entirely put aside. Sometimes he tried over a few measures on the piano as many as fifty times, changing the value or significance of a note; as a result, his piano writing is almost always "pianistic." In one respect he was sometimes careless: in the noting of the expression marks. By the time he arrived at that duty he was usually tired out. For this reason, much in his printed music is marked differently from the way he actually played it in concert. He never, in performance, changed a note, save in a few of the earlier pieces; but in details of expression he often departed widely from the printed directions.

He was always profoundly absorbed when at work, though not to the extent of being able to

compose amid noise or disturbance. He needed
to isolate himself as much as possible; although,
when it could not be avoided, he contrived to
work effectively under obstructive conditions;
the Largo of the "Sonata Tragica," for example,
was written in Boston when he was harassed by
drudgery and care. During the earlier days at
Peterboro he composed in a music room which
was joined to the main body of the house by a
covered passage; in this way he could hear
nothing of the household workings, and was
unaware of the chance caller. No one was ever
allowed to intrude upon him, save his wife. Yet
certain outside noises were still apparent; so the
log cabin in the woods was built. There he used
to go nearly every morning, coming home when
he felt disposed, and usually going to the golf
grounds for a game before dinner, which he
always had at night. He kept a piano in the
music room as well as at the log cabin; so if he
felt like working in the evening he could do so;
and when he was especially engrossed he often
worked into the small hours. His unselfishness
made it easy for his wife, when she deemed a
change and rest essential, to make the excuse
that *she* needed it. After a preliminary protest
he would usually give in, and they would leave
Peterboro for a few days' excursion.

He knew discouragement in an extreme form. Many weeks, even months, had to pass before his discontent over the last child of his imagination would become normal. Particularly was this so with the larger works; though each one was started in a fever of inspiration, a longing to reduce to actual form the impossible. He was always disheartened when a work was finished, but he was too sane in his judgment not to have moments when he could estimate fairly the quality of what he had written. But those were rare moments; as a rule, it was in his future music that he was always going to do his "really good work," and he longed ardently for leisure and freedom from care, so that, as he once bitterly said, he would not have to press into a small piano piece material enough to make a movement of a symphony.

His preferences in the matter of his own music were not very definite. In 1903, when he had finished all that he was to write, he expressed a preference for the "Dirge" from the "Indian" suite above anything that he had composed. "Of all my music," he confessed at this time, "the 'Dirge' in the 'Indian' suite pleases me most. It affects me deeply and did when I was writing it. In it an Indian woman laments the death of her son; but to me, as I wrote it, it seemed to express a world-sorrow rather than a particularised grief." His estimate of the value of the music has, naturally, no extraordinary importance; but my conviction is that, in this instance, his judgment was correct. As to the sonatas, he cared most for the "Keltic"; after that, for the "Eroica," as a whole; though I doubt whether there was anything in the two that he cared for quite as he did for the Largo in the "'Tragica" and certain parts of the "Norse." He felt concerning the "Keltic" that there was hardly a bar in it that he wanted changed, that he had scarcely ever written any thing so rounded, so complete, in which the joining was so invisible. He played it *con amore*, and it grew to be part of himself as no other of his works ever did. Technically, it was never hard for him, whereas he found the "Eroica" exhausting, physically and mentally.

Of the smaller works he preferred the "Sea Pieces," as a whole, above all the others; yet there were single things in each of the other sets for which he cared perhaps as much. Of the "Sea Pieces" those he liked best were: "To the Sea," "From the Depths," "In Mid-Ocean"; of the "Fireside Tales": the "Haunted House," "Salamander," "'Brer Rabbit"; and he had a tender feeling for "In a German Forest," which always seemed to bring back the Frankfort days to his memory. Of the "New England Idyls," his favorites were: "In Deep Woods," "Mid-Winter," "From a Log Cabin."

In his composition he was growing away from piano work, — he felt that the future must mean larger, probably orchestral, forms, for him, and his dream of an ultimate leisure was a dream for which his friends can be thankful. He did not end with despair at his heart that the distracting work, the yearly drudgery, were to go on forever.

His preferences in music were governed by the independence which characterised his intellectual judgments. Of the moderns, Wagner was his god; for Liszt he had an unbounded admiration, though he detected the showman, the mere juggler, in him; Tchaikovsky stirred him mightily; Brahms did not as a rule give him pleasure, though certain of that master's more fertile moments compelled his appreciation. Grieg he delighted in. To him he dedicated both his "Norse" and "Keltic" sonatas. In response to his request for permission to inscribe the first of these to his eminent contemporary, he received from Grieg the following delectable letter — one of the Norwegian's very few attempts at English composition (I quote it verbatim; the spelling is Grieg's): —

Copenhagen 26/10/99
Hotel King of Denmark.

My dear Sir!

Will you permit
me in bad English to
express my best thanks
for your kind letter and
for the sympathi. you
feel for my music.
Of course it will be
a great honor and plea-
sure for me to accept
your dedication.
Some years ago I
thought it possible
to shake hand with

you in your own country. But unfortunately my delicate health does not seem to agree. At all events, if we are not to meet, I am glad to read in the papers of your artistical success in America. With my best wishes, I am, dear sir, yours very truly

Evard Grieg

ACCEPTING THE DEDICATION OF THE "NORSE"
ENGLISH COMPOSITION (SEE PAGE 73)

COPENHAGEN, 26/10/99.
Hotel King of Denmark.

MY DEAR SIR!

Will you remit me in bad English to express my best thanks for your kind letter and for the sympathi you feel for my music. Of course it will be a great honor and pleasure for me to accept your dedication.

Some years ago I thought it possible to shake hands with you in your own country. But unfortunately my delicat health does not seem to agree. At all events, if we are not to meet, I am glad to read in the papers of your artistical success in Amerika.

With my best wishes,

I am, dear Sir,

Yours very truly,

EDVARD GRIEG.

I may quote also, in this place, because of its unusual interest, a letter written (in German) by Grieg to Mrs. MacDowell when he learned of her husband's collapse: —

CHRISTIANIA,
December 14, 1905.

DEAR MADAM:

The news of MacDowell's serious illness has deeply affected me. Permit me therefore to express to you my own and my wife's sincerest sympathy for you. I am a great admirer of MacDowell's Muse, and would regard it as a severe blow if his best creative period should be so hastily broken off. From all that I hear of your husband, his qualities as a man are as remarkable as his qualities as an artist. He is a complete Personality, with an unusually sympathetic and sensitive nervous system. Such a temperament gives one the capacity not only for moods of the highest transport, but for an unspeakable sorrow tenfold more profound. This is the unsolvable riddle.   An artist so ideally endowed [*ein so ideal ange-legter Künstler*] as MacDowell must ask himself: Why have I received from nature this delicately strung lyre, if I were better off without it? So unmerciful is Life that every artist must ask himself this question. The only consolation is: Work — yes, even the severest labours. . . . *But:* the artist is an optimist. Otherwise he would be no artist. He believes and hopes in the triumph of the good and the beautiful. He trusts in his lucky star till his last breath. And you, the wife of a highly gifted artist, will not and must not lose hope! In similar cases, happily, one often witnesses a seemingly inexplicable recovery. If it can give MacDowell a moment's cheer, say to him that he has in distant Norway a warm and understanding friend who feels for him, and wishes from his heart that for him, as for you, better times may soon come.

With best greeting to you both,

Your respectful

EDVARD GRIEG.

MacDowell's feeling in regard to Strauss, whom he considered to have developed what he called the "suggestive" (delineative) power of music at the expense of its finer potentialities, is indicated in a lecture which he prepared on the subject of "Suggestion in Music." "'Thus Spake

Zarathustra,'" he wrote, "may be considered the apotheosis of this power of suggestion in tonal colour, and in it I believe we can see the tendency I allude to [the tendency "to elevate what should be a means of adding power and intensity to musical speech, to the importance of musical speech itself"]. It stuns by its glorious magnificence of tonal texture. The suggestion, at the beginning, of the rising sun, is a mighty example of the overwhelming power of tone-colour. The upward sweep of the music to the highest regions of light has something splendrous about it; and yet I remember once hearing in London a song sung in the street at night that seemed to me to contain a truer germ of music." — From which it will be seen that there were limits to the æsthetic sympathy of even so liberal and divining an appreciator as MacDowell.

The modern Frenchmen he knew scarcely at all. Some of d'Indy's earlier music he had heard and admired; but that he would have cared for such a score as Debussy's "La Mer" I very much doubt. I remember his amusement over what he called the "queerness" of a sonata by the Belgian Lekeu for violin and piano, which he had read or heard. It is likely that he would have found little to attract him in the more characteristic music of d'Indy, Debussy, and

Ravel; his instincts and temperament led him into a wholly different region of expression. He was a prophet of modernity; but it was a modernity that he alone exemplifies: it has no exact parallel.

Concerning the classics he had his own views. Of Bach he wrote that he believed him to have accomplished his work as "one of the world's mightiest tone-poets not by means of the contrapuntal methods of his day, but in spite of them. The laws of canon and fugue are based upon as prosaic a foundation as those of the Rondo and Sonata Form, and I find it impossible to imagine their ever having been a spur, an incentive, to poetic musical speech."

Of Mozart he wrote: "It is impossible to forget the fact that in his piano works he was first and foremost a piano virtuoso, a child prodigy: of whom filigree work (we cannot call this Orientalism, for it was more or less of German pattern, traced from the *fioriture* of the Italian opera singer) was expected by the public for which his sonatas were written. . . . We need freshness and sincerity in forming our judgments of art. . . . If we read on one page of some history (every history of music has such a page) that Mozart's sonatas are sublime; that they far transcend anything written for the harpsichord or clavichord by Haydn or his contemporaries, we are apt to echo the saying . . . But let us look the thing straight in the face: Mozart's sonatas are compositions entirely unworthy of the author of 'The Magic Flute' and 'Don Giovanni,' or of any composer with pretensions to more than mediocre talent. They are written in a style of flashy harpsichord virtuosity such as Liszt in his most despised moments never descended to. Yet I am well aware that this statement would be dismissed as either absurd or heretical, according to the point of view of the particular objector."

Of Mendelssohn he said: "Mendelssohn professed to be an 'absolutist' in music. As a matter of fact, he stands on the same ground that Liszt and Berlioz did; for almost everything he wrote, even to the smallest piano piece, he furnished with an explanatory title. . . . Formalist though he was, his work often exhibits eccentricities of form — as, for instance, in the Scotch Symphony, where, in the so-called 'exposition' of the first movement, he throws in an extra little theme that laps over his frame with a jaunty disregard of the rules that is delightful. . . . His technic of piano writing was perfect; compared with Beethoven's it was a revelation. He never committed the fault of mere virtuoso writing, which is remarkable when we consider how strong a temptation there must have been to do so. In his piano music can be found the germs of most of the pianistic innovations that are usually identified with other composers — for instance, the manner of enveloping the melody with runs, the discovery of which has been ascribed to Thalberg, but which we find in Mendelssohn's first Prelude, written in 1833. The interlocking passages which have become so prevalent in modern music we find in his compositions dating from 1835."

Of Schumann he said happily: "His music is not avowed programme-music; neither is it, as was much of Schubert's, pure delight in beautiful sound. It did not break through formalism by sheer violence of emotion, as did Beethoven's: it represents the rhapsodical revery of an inspired poet to whom no imaginative vagary seems strange or alien, and who has the faculty of relating his visions, never attempting to give them coherence, and unaware of their character until perhaps when, awakened from his dream, he naïvely wonders what they may have meant — you remember that he added titles to his music after it was composed. He put his dreams in music and guessed their meaning afterward."

Of Liszt and Chopin: "To all of this new, strange music [the piano music of the Romantics] Liszt and Chopin added the wonderful tracery of

Orientalism. The difference between these two is, that with Chopin this tracery developed poetic thought as with a thin gauze; whereas with Liszt [in his piano music] the embellishment itself made the starting-point for almost a new art in tonal combination, the effects of which one sees on every hand to-day. To realise its influence one need only compare the easy mastery of the arabesque displayed in the simplest piano piece of to-day with the awkward and gargoyle-like figuration of Beethoven and his predecessors. We may justly attribute this to Liszt rather than to Chopin, whose nocturne embellishments are but first cousins to those of the Englishman, John Field."

Of Wagner: "His music-dramas, shorn of the fetters of the actual spoken word, emancipated from the materialism of acting, painting, and furniture, must be considered the greatest achievement in our art."

Concerning Form in music, he observed: "If by the word 'form' our purists meant the most poignant expression of poetic thought in music, if they meant by this term the art of arranging musical sounds so that they constituted the most telling presentation of a musical idea, I should have nothing to say. But as it is, the word in almost its invariable use by theorists stands for what are

called 'stoutly-built periods,' 'subsidiary themes'
and the like, a happy combination of which in
certain prescribed keys is supposed to constitute
good form.   Such a principle, inherited from the
necessities and fashions of the dance, and changing from time to time, is surely not worthy of the
strange worship it has received.   In their eagerness to press this great revolutionist [Beethoven]
into their own ranks in the fight of narrow theory
against expansion and progress, the most amusing
mistakes are constantly occurring.   For example,
the first movement of this sonata [the so-called
"Moonlight"] — which, as we know, is a poem
of profound sorrow and the most poignant resignation alternating with despair — has, by some
strange torturing, been cited as being in strict
sonata-form by one theorist (Harding: Novello's
primer), is dubbed a free fantasy by another
(Matthews), and is described as being in song-
form by another: all of which is somewhat weak-
ened by the dictum of still another theorist that
the music is absolutely formless! A form of so
doubtful an identity can surely lay small claim to
any serious intellectual value. . . . In our modern
days we too often, Procrustes-like, make our
ideas to fit the forms.   We put our guest, the
poetic thought, that comes to us like a homing
bird from out of the mystery of the blue sky —

we put this confiding stranger straightway into that iron bed: the 'sonata-form' — or perhaps even the 'third-rondo form,' for we have quite an assortment; and should the idea survive, and grow, and become too large for the bed, and if we have grown to love it too much to cut off its feet and thus *make* it fit (as did that old robber of Attica), why then we run the risk of having some wiseacre say, as is said of Chopin: 'Yes — but he is weak in sonata-form'! . . . Form should be nothing more than a synonym for *coherence*. No idea, whether great or small, can find utterance without form; but that form will be inherent in the idea, and there will be as many forms as there are adequately expressed ideas in the world."

Concerning programme-music he wrote at length. "In my opinion," he says in one of his lectures, "the battle over what music can express and what it cannot express has been carried on wrong lines. We are always referred back to language as actually expressing an idea, when, as a matter of fact, language expresses nothing but that which its vital parallel means of expression, gesture and facial expression, permit it to express. Words mean nothing whatsoever in themselves; the same words in different languages mean wholly different things; for written words

are mere symbols, and no more express things or
ideas than any marks on paper would. Yet language is forever striving to emulate music by
actually expressing something, besides merely
symbolising it, and thus we have in poetry the
coining of onomatopoetic words — words that
will bring the things they stand for more vividly
before our eyes and minds. Now music may
express all that words can express and much
more, for it is the natural means of expression
for all animals, mankind included. If musical
sounds were accepted as symbols for things we
would have another speech. It seems strange to
say that by means of music one could say the
most commonplace thing, as, for instance: 'I am
going to take a walk'; yet this is precisely what the
Chinese have been doing for centuries. For such
things, however, our word-symbols do perfectly
well, and such a symbolising of musical sounds
must detract, I think, from the high mission of
music: which, as I conceive, is neither to be an
agent for expressing material things; nor to utter
pretty sounds to amuse the ear; nor a sensuous
excitant to fire the blood, or a sedative to lull the
senses: it is a *language*, but a language of the intangible, a kind of soul-language. It appeals
directly to the *Seelenzustände* it springs from, for
it is the natural expression of it, rather than, like

words, a translation of it into set stereotyped symbols which may or may not be accepted for what they were intended to denote by the writer" — a *credo* which sums up in fairly complete form his theory of music-making, whatever validity it may have as a philosophical generalisation.

In regard to the sadly vexed question of musical nationalism, especially in its relation to America, his position was definite and positive. His views on this subject may well be quoted somewhat in detail, since they have not always been justly represented or fully understood. In the following excerpt, from a lecture on "Folk-Music," he pays his respects to Dvořák's "New World" symphony, and touches upon his own attitude toward the case as exemplified in his "Indian" suite:

"A man is generally something different from the clothes he wears or the business he is occupied with; but when we do see a man identified with his clothes we think but little of him. And so it is with music. So-called Russian, Bohemian, or any other purely national music has no place in art, for its characteristics may be duplicated by anyone who takes the fancy to do so. On the other hand, the vital element of music — personality — stands alone. We have seen the Viennese Strauss family adopting the cross rhythms of the Spanish — or, to be more accurate, the Moorish or Arab—school of art.　Moszkowski the Pole writes Spanish dances.　Cowen in England writes a Scandinavian Symphony.　Grieg the Norwegian writes Arabian music; and, to cap the climax, we have here in America been offered a pattern for an 'American' national musical costume by the Bohemian Dvořák — though what the Negro melodies have to do with Americanism in art still remains a mystery. Music that can be made by 'recipe' is not music, but 'tailoring.'　To be sure, this tailoring may serve to cover a beautiful thought; but — why cover it? and, worst of all, why cover it (if covered it must be: if the trademark of nationality is indispensable, which I deny) — why cover it with the badge of whilom slavery rather than with the stern but at least manly and free rudeness of the North American Indian?　If what is called local tone colour is necessary to music (which it most emphatically is not), why not adopt some of the Hindoo *Ragas* and modes — each one of which (and the modes alone number over seventy-two) will give an individual tonal character to the music written according to its rules? But the means of 'creating' a national music to which I have alluded are childish.　No: before a people can find a musical writer to echo its

genius it must first possess men who truly represent it — that is to say, men who, being part of
the people, love the country for itself: men who
put into their music what the nation has put into
its life; and in the case of America it needs above
all, both on the part of the public and on the
part of the writer, absolute freedom from the
restraint that an almost unlimited deference to
European thought and prejudice has imposed
upon us.   Masquerading in the so-called nationalism of Negro clothes cut in Bohemia will not help
us.   What we must arrive at is the youthful
optimistic vitality and the undaunted tenacity of
spirit that characterizes the American man.
This is what I hope to see echoed in American
music."

Of MacDowell as a pianist, Mr. Henry T.
Finck, who had known him in this capacity
almost from the beginning of his career in America,
has written for me his impressions, and I shall
quote them, rather than any of my own; since I
had comparatively few opportunities to hear him
display, at his best, the full measure of his ability:

"As he never felt quite sure," writes Mr. Finck,
"that what he was composing was worth while, so,
in the matter of playing in public, he was so self-
distrustful that when he came on the stage and
sat down on the piano stool he hung his head and

looked a good deal like a school-boy detected in the act of doing something he ought not to do.

"Often though I was with him — sometimes a week at a time in Peterboro — I never could persuade him to play for me. I once asked Paderewski to play for me his new set of songs, and he promptly did so. But MacDowell always was 'out of practice,' or had some other excuse, generally a witticism or bit of sarcasm at his own expense. I am sorry now that I did not urge him with more persistence, for he might have yielded in the end, and I would have got a more *intime* idea of his playing; for after all a musical tête-à-tête like that is preferable to any public hearing. I never heard Grieg play at a concert, but I am sure that the hour I sat near him in his Bergen home, while he played and his wife sang, gave me a better appreciation of his skill as an interpreter than I could have got in a public hall with an audience to distract his attention. One afternoon I called on Saint-Saëns at his hotel after one of his concerts in New York. Talking about it, he sat down at the piano, ran over his *Valse Canariote*, and said: 'That's the way I *ought* to have played it!'

"MacDowell was quite right in saying that he was out of practice; he generally was, his duties as professor allowing him little time for technical exercising; but once every few years he set to work and got his fingers into a condition which enabled them to follow his intentions; and those intentions, it is needless to say, were always honourable! He never played any of those show pieces which help along a pianist, but confined himself to the best he could find.

"Usually the first half of a recital was devoted to the classical and romantic masters, the second to his own compositions. Beethoven, Schubert, Chopin, Liszt, Grieg, were likely to be represented, and he also did missionary work for Templeton Strong and other Americans. His interpretation of the music of other composers was both objective and subjective; there was no distortion or exaggeration, yet one could not mistake the fact that it was MacDowell who was playing it.

"The expression, 'he played like a composer,' is often used to hint that the technic was not that of a virtuoso. In this sense MacDowell did not play like a composer; his technical skill was equal to everything he played, though never obtrusive. In another sense he did play 'like a composer,' especially when interpreting his own pieces; that is, he played with an insight, a subtlety of expression, which only a creative performer has at his command. I doubt if Chopin himself could have rendered one of his pieces with more ravishing delicacy than MacDowell showed in playing his 'To a Wild Rose.' I doubt if Liszt could have shown a more overwhelming dramatic power than MacDowell did in playing his 'Keltic' sonata. In this combination of feminine tenderness with masculine strength he was, as in his creative gift, a man of genius. After one of his concerts I wrote in the glow of enthusiasm that I would rather hear him than any pianist in the field excepting Paderewski; that utterance I never saw reason to modify."

For an interesting and closely observed description of MacDowell's technical peculiarities as a piano player I am indebted to his friend and pupil, Mr. T. P. Currier, who had followed Mac-Dowell's career as a pianist from the time of his first public appearance in Boston:

"[His finger velocity] was at that time [in 1888] the most striking characteristic of his playing," says Mr. Currier. "For him, too, it was a mere bagatelle. He took to prestissimo like a duck to water. He could, in fact, play fast more easily than he could slowly. One of his ever-present fears was that in performance his fingers would run away with him. And many hours were spent in endeavours to control such an embarrassing tendency. This extraordinary velocity, acquired in the Paris Conservatory, and from his friend and teacher, Carl Heymann, of Frankfort, invariably set his listeners agape, and was always one of the chief sensations at his concerts.

"But for this finger speeding and for his other technical acquirements as well, MacDowell cared little, except as they furthered his one absorbing aim. He was heart and soul a composer, and to be able to play his own music as he heard it in his inner ear was his single spur to practice. From the time of his complete immersion in composition, his ideas of pianistic effects, of tone colour, gradually led him farther and farther away from conventional pianism. Scales and arpeggios, as commonly rendered, had no longer interest or charm for him. He cared for finger passages only when they could be made to suggest what he wanted them to suggest in his own colour-scheme. With his peculiar touch and facility at command, he rejoiced in turning such passages into streams and swirls of tone, marked with strong accents and coloured with vivid, dynamic contrasts.

"That his passage playing rarely sounded clean and pure — like that of a Rosenthal — was due not only to his musical predilections, but to his hand formation as well. His hand was broad and rather thick-set, and tremendously muscular.

It would not bend back at the knuckles; and the fingers also had no well-defined knuckle movement. It appears, therefore, that he could not, if he would, have succeeded on more conventional technical lines. Gradually he developed great strength and intense activity in the middle joints, which enabled him to play with a very close, often overlapping, touch, and to maintain extremely rapid tempi in legato or staccato with perfect ease and little fatigue. With this combination of velocity and close touch, it was a slight matter to produce those pianistic effects which were especially dear to him.

"MacDowell's finger development has been thus dwelt upon, because it was, as has been said, the feature of his technic which immediately surprised and captivated his hearers. Less noticeable was his wrist and octave work. But his chord playing, though also relatively unattractive, was even in those early days almost as uncommon in its way as was his velocity. And in this field of technic, during his later years, when in composition his mind turned almost wholly to this mode of expression, he reached a plane of tonal effect which, for variety, from vague, shadowy, mysterious *ppp*, to virile, orchestral *ffff*, has never been surpassed by any pianist who has visited these shores in recent years. His tone in chord

THE HOUSE AT PETERBORO, NEW HAMPSHIRE, WHERE MACDOWELL SPENT HIS SUMMERS

THE PIAZZA AND GARDEN WALK AT PETERBORO

playing, it is true, was often harsh, and this fault also appeared in his melodic delivery. But in both cases any unmusical effect was so greatly overbalanced by many rare and beautiful qualities of tone production, that it was easily forgiven and forgotten.

"Wonderful tone blending in finger passages; a peculiarly crisp, yet veiled staccato; chord playing extraordinary in variety, — tender, mysterious, sinister, heroic; a curiously unconventional yet effective melodic delivery; playing replete with power, vitality, and dramatic significance, always forcing upon the ear the phrase, never the tickling of mere notes; a really marvellous command and use of both pedals, — these were the characteristics of MacDowell's pianistic art as he displayed it in the exposition of his own works. Unquestionably he was. a born pianist. If it had not been for his genius for composition, he would, without doubt, have been known as a brilliant and forceful interpreter of the greatest piano literature. But his compositional bent turned him completely away from mere piano playing. He was a composer-pianist, and as such he ever desired to be regarded."

As a pianist, as in all other matters touching his own capacities, he was often tortured by doubts concerning the effect of his performances.

"I shall never forget," recalls his wife, "the first time he played it [the "Eroica" sonata] in Boston. We all thought he did it wonderfully. But when I went around to the green-room door to find him, fearing something might be wrong, as he had not come to me, he had gone. When I got home, accompanied by two friends, there he was almost in a corner, white, and as if he were guilty of some crime, and he said as we came in: 'I can play better than that. But I was so tired!' We almost wept with the pity of the unnecessary suffering, which was yet so real and intense. In a short time he was more himself, and naïvely admitted that he had played three movements well, but had been a 'd—— fool in one.' I grew to be very used to this as the years went on, for he could not help emphasizing to himself what he did badly, and ignoring the good."

He left few uncompleted works. There are among his manuscripts three movements of a symphony, two movements of a suite for string orchestra, a suite for violin and piano, some songs and piano pieces, and a large number of sketches. He had schemes for a music-drama on an Arthurian subject, and sketched a single act of it. He had planned this work upon novel lines: there was to be comparatively little singing, and much emphasis was to be laid upon the orchestral commentary; the action was to be carried on by a combination of pantomime and tableaux, and the scenic element was to be conspicuous — a suggestion which he got in part from E. A. Abbey's Holy Grail frescoes in the Boston Public Library. But he had determined to write his own text: and the prospective labour of this, made more formidable by his restricted leisure, finally discouraged him, and he abandoned the project. Five years before his death he destroyed the sketches that he had made; only a few fragments remain.

A rare and admirable man! — a man who would have been a remarkable personality if he had not written a note of music. His faults — and he was far from being a paragon — were never petty or contemptible: they were truly the defects of his qualities — of his honesty, his courage, his passionate and often reckless zeal in the promotion of what he believed to be sound and fine in art and in life. Mr. Philip Hale, whose long friendship with MacDowell gives him the right to speak with peculiar authority, and whose habit is that of sobriety in speech, has written of him in words whose justice and felicity cannot be bettered: "A man of blameless life, he was never pharasaical; he was compassionate toward the slips and failings of poor humanity. He was a true patriot, proud and hopeful of his country and of its artistic future, but he could not brook the thought of patriotism used as a cloak to cover mediocrity in art. . . . He was one who worked steadily and courageously in the face of discouragement; who never courted by trickery or device the favour of the public; who never fawned upon those who might help him; who in his art kept himself pure and un-spotted."

"O that so many pitchers of rough clay
Should prosper and the porcelain break in two!"

THE MUSIC–MAKER

A WINTER VIEW OF THE PETERBORO HOUSE

THE MUSIC-MAKER

CHAPTER III

HIS ART AND ITS METHODS

AMONG those music-makers of to-day who are both pre-eminent and representative the note of sincere romance is infrequently sounded. The fact must be obvious to the most casual observer of musical art in its contemporary development. The significant work of the most considerable musicians of our time — of Strauss, Debussy, Loeffler, d'Indy — has few essentially romantic characteristics. It is necessary to distinguish between that fatuous Romanticism of which Mr. Ernest Newman has given an unequalled definition: the Romanticism which expended itself in the fabrication of a pasteboard world of "gloomy forests, enchanted castles, impossible maidens, and the obsolete profession of magic," and that other and imperishable Spirit of Romance whose infrequent embodiment in modern music I have remarked. *That* is a romance in no wise divorced from reality — is, in fact, but reality diviningly perceived; if it uses the old Romanticistic properties, it uses them not because of any

inherent validity which they possess, but because
they may at times be made to serve as symbols.
It deals in a truth that is no less authentic because
it is conveyed in terms of a beauty that may
often be in the last degree incalculable and
aërial.

It is to its persistent embodiment of this valid
spirit of romance that MacDowell's work owes its
final and particular distinction. I know of no
composer who has displayed a like sensitiveness
to the finer stuff of romance. He has chosen
more than occasionally to employ, in the accomplishment of his purposes, what seems at first to
be precisely the magical apparatus so necessary
to the older Romanticism. Dryads and elves
are his intimate companions, and he dwells at
times under fairy boughs and in enchanted woods;
but for him, as for the poets of the Celtic tradition, these things are but the manifest images of
an interior passion and delight. Seen in the
transfiguring mirror of his music, the moods and
events of the natural world, and of the drama
that plays incessantly in the hearts of men, are
vivified into shapes and designs of irresistible
beauty and appeal. He is of those quickened
ministers of beauty who attest for us the reality
of that changeless and timeless loveliness which
the visible world of the senses and the invisible

world of the imagination are ceaselessly revealing
to the simple of heart, the dream-filled, and the
unwise.

MacDowell presents throughout the entire
body of his work the noteworthy spectacle of a
radical without extravagance, a musician at once
in accord with, and detached from, the dominant
artistic movement of his day. The observation
is more a definition than an encomium. He is a
radical in that, to his sense, music is nothing if
not articulate. Wagner's luminous phrase, "the
fertilisation of music by poetry," would have
implied for him no mere æsthetic abstraction, but
an intimate and ever-present ideal. He was a
musician, yet he looked out upon the visible
world and inward upon the world of the emotions
through the transforming eyes of the poet. He
would have none of a formal and merely decora-
tive beauty — a beauty serving no expressional
need of the heart or the imagination. In this
ultimate sense he is to be regarded as a realist — a
realist with the romantic's vision, the romantic's
preoccupation; and yet he is as alien to the frequently unleavened literalism of Richard Strauss
as he is to the academic ideal. Though he
conceives the prime mission of music to be in-
terpretive, he insists no less emphatically that,
in its function as an expressional instrument,

it shall concern itself with essences and impressions, and not at all with transcriptions. His standpoint is, in the last analysis, that of the poet rather than of the typical musician: the standpoint of the poet intent mainly upon a vivid embodiment of the quintessence of personal vision and emotion, who has elected to utter that truth and that emotion in terms of musical beauty. One is, indeed, almost tempted to say that he is paramountly a poet, to whom the supplementary gift of musical speech has been extravagantly vouchsafed.

He is a realist, as I have said — applying the term in that larger sense which denotes the transmutation of life into visible or audible form, and which implicates Beethoven as well as Wagner, Schumann as well as Liszt, Tchaikovsky and Debussy as well as Strauss: all those in whom the desire for intelligible utterance coexists with, or supersedes, the impulse toward perfected design. But if MacDowell's method of transmutation is not the method of Strauss, neither is it the method of Schumann, or of Debussy. He occupies a middle ground between the undaunted literalism of the Munich tone-poet and the sentimental posturings into which the romanticism of Schumann so frequently declined. It is impossible to conceive him attempting the musical exposition of such themes as kindled the imagination of Strauss when he wrought out his "Heldenleben," "Zarathustra," and "Till Eulenspiegel"; nor has he any appreciable affinity with the prismatic subtleties of the younger French school: so that there is little in the accent of his musical speech to remind one of the representative voices of modernity.

Though he has avoided shackling his music to a detailed programme, he has never very seriously espoused the sophistical compromise which concedes the legitimacy of programme-music provided it speaks as potently to one who does not know the subject-matter as to one who does. The bulk of his music no more discloses its full measure of beauty and eloquence to one who is in ignorance of its poetic basis than would Wagner's "Faust" overture, Tchaikovsky's "Romeo and Juliet," or Debussy's "L'Après-midi d'un Faune." Its appeal is conditioned upon an understanding of the basis of drama and emotional crisis upon which the musician has built; and in much of his music he has frankly recognized this fact, and has printed at the beginning of such works as the "Idyls" and "Poems" after Goethe and Heine, the "Norse" and "Keltic" sonatas, the "Sea Pieces," and the "New England Idyls," the fragment of verse or legend or meditation which has served as the particular stimulus of his inspiration; while in other works he has contented himself with the suggestion of a mood or subject embodied in his title, as, for example, in his "Woodland Sketches," — "To a Wild Rose," "Will o' the Wisp," "At an Old Trysting Place," "In Autumn," "From an Indian Lodge," "To a Water-Lily," "A Deserted Farm." That he has been tempted, however, in the direction of the compromise to which I have alluded, is evident from the fact that although his symphonic poem "Lancelot and Elaine" is built upon the frame of an extremely definite sequence of events, — such as Lancelot's downfall in the tournament, his return to the court, Guinevere's casting away of the trophies, the approach of the barge bearing Elaine's body, and Lancelot's reverie by the river bank, — he gives in the published score no hint whatever of the particular phases of that moving chronicle of passion and tragedy which he has so faithfully striven to represent. "I would never have insisted," he wrote in 1899, "that this symphonic poem need mean 'Lancelot and Elaine' to everyone. It did to me, however, and in the hope that my artistic enjoyment might be shared by others, I added the title to my music."

But if MacDowell displayed at times the usual inconsistency of the modern tone-poet in his attitude toward the whole subject of programme-music,* the tendency was neither a persistent nor

* That MacDowell came later to realise the disadvantages, no less than the inconsistency, of writing programme-music based upon a detailed and definite programme and then withholding the programme, is indicated by this passage from a lecture on Beethoven which he delivered at Columbia: "If it [Beethoven's music] is absolute music, according to the accepted meaning of the term, either it must be beautiful music in itself, — that is, composed of beautiful sounds, — or its excuse for *not* being beautiful must rest upon its power of expressing emotions and ideas that demand other than merely beautiful tones for their utterance. Music, for instance, that would give us the emotion — if I may call it that — of a series of exploding bombshells could hardly be called 'absolute music'; yet that is exactly what the opening of the last movement of the so-called 'Moonlight' Sonata meant to Miss Thackeray, who speaks of it in her story, 'Beauty and the Beast.' . . . If this is abstract music, it is bad. We know, however, that Beethoven had some poetic idea in his mind as he wrote this; but as he never gave the clew to the world, the music has been swallowed as 'absolute music' by the modern formalists" — a comment which would apply almost word for word, with a change of names and titles, to a certain tumultuous and "unbeautiful" passage in Mac-Dowell's "Lancelot and Elaine." This passage is intended to express the rage and jealousy of Guinevere; but Mac-Dowell has given no indication of this fact in his score, and only occasionally does the information find its way into the programme-books. Yet in his own copy of the score he wrote a complete and detailed key to the significance of the music at every point. Such are the ways of the musical realist!

determined one; and he was, as I have noted, even less disposed toward the frankly literal methods of which Strauss and his followers are such invincible exponents. His nearest approach to such diverting expedients as the bleating sheep and the exhilarating wind-machine of "Don Quixote" is in the denotement of the line:

"And like a thunderbolt he falls"

in his graphic paraphrase of Tennyson's poem, "The Eagle" — an indulgence which the most exigent champion of programmatic reserve would probably condone. In the main, MacDowell's predilection for what he chose to call "suggestive" music finds expression in such continent symbolism as he employs in those elastically wrought tone-poems, brief or vigorously sustained, in which he sets forth a poetic concept with memorable vividness — in such things as his terse though astonishingly eloquent apostrophe "To a Wandering Iceberg," and his "In Mid-Ocean," from the "Sea Pieces"; in "To a Water-lily," from the "Woodland Sketches"; in the "Winter" and "In Deep Woods" from the "New England Idyls"; in the "Marionettes" ("Soubrette," "Lover," "Witch," "Clown," "Villain," "Sweetheart"); in the Raff-like orchestral suite, op. 42 ("In a Haunted Forest,"

"Summer Idyll," "The Shepherdess' Song,"
"Forest Spirits"), and in the later and far more
important "Indian" suite for orchestra ("Legend," "Love Song," "In War-time," "Dirge,"
"Village Festival").

He was, in an extraordinarily complete sense, a
celebrant of the natural world. His imagination
was enslaved by the miraculous pageant of the
visible earth, and he sought tirelessly to transfix
some moment of its wonder or its splendour
or its terror in permanent images of tone. The
melancholy beauty of the autumn woods, the
loveliness of quiet waters under fading skies,
the sapphire and emerald glories, or the ominous
chantings, of the sea, the benign and mysterious
majesty of summer stars, the lyric sweetness of a
meadow: these things urged him to musical
transcripts, notations of loving tenderness and
sincerity. His music is redolent of the breath
and odour of woodland places, of lanes and moors
and gardens; or it is saturated with salt spray;
or it communicates the incommunicable in its
voicing of that indefinable and evanescent sense
of association which is evoked by certain aspects,
certain phases, of the outer world — that sudden
emotion of things past and irrecoverable which
may cling about a field at sunset, or a quiet
street at dusk, or a sudden intimation of spring
in the scent of lilacs.

But although such themes as he loved to dwell upon in his celebration of the magic of the natural world were very precious to his imagination, the human spectacle held for him, from the first, an emotion scarcely less swift and abundant. His scope is comprehensive: he can voice the archest gaiety, a naïve and charming humour, as in the "Marionettes" and in the songs "From an Old Garden"; there is passion in the symphonic poems and in many of the songs; while in the sonatas and in the "Indian" suite the tragic note is struck with impressive and indubitable authority.

Of the specifically musical traits in which MacDowell exhibits the tendencies and preferences which underlie his art, one must begin by saying that his distinguishing quality — that which puts so unmistakable a stamp upon his work — eludes precise definition. His tone is unmistakable. Its chief possession is a certain clarity and directness which is apparent no less in moments of great stress and complexity of emotion than in passages of simpler and slighter content. His style has little of the torrential rhetoric, the unbridled gusto and exuberance of Strauss, though it owns something of his forthright quality; nor has it any of Debussy's withdrawals. One thinks, as a discerning commentator has observed, of the "broad Shakespearian daylight" of Fitzgerald's fine phrase as being not inapplicable to the atmosphere of MacDowell's writing. He has few reservations, and he shows small liking for recondite effects of harmonic colour, for the wavering melodic line — which is far from implying that he is ever merely obvious or banal: that he never is. His clarity, his directness, find issue in an order of expression at once lucid and distinguished, at once spontaneous and expressive. It is difficult to recall, in any example of his maturer work, a single passage that is not touched with a measure of beauty and character. He had, of course, his period of crude experimentation, his days of discipleship. In his earlier writing there is not a little that is unworthy of him: much in which one seeks vainly for that note of distinction and personality which sounds so constantly throughout the finer body of his work. But in that considerable portion of his output which is genuinely representative — say from his opus 45 onward — he sustains his art upon a noteworthy level of fineness and strength.

The range of his expressional gamut is striking. One is at a loss to say whether he is happier in emotional moments of weighty significance, — as in many pages of the sonatas and some of the "Sea Pieces," — or in such cameo-like perform-

ances as the "Woodland Sketches," certain of the
"Marionettes,"* and the exquisite song group,
"From an Old Garden," in which he attains an
order of delicate eloquence difficult to associate
with the mind which shaped the heroic ardours
of the "Norse" and "Keltic" sonatas. His capacity for forceful utterance is remarkable. Only
in certain pages of Strauss is there anything in
contemporary music which compares, for superb
virility, dynamic power, and sweep of line, with
the opening of the "Keltic" sonata. He has,
moreover, a remarkable gift for compact expression. Time and again he astonishes by his
ability to charge a composition of the briefest
span with an emotional or dramatic content of
large and far-reaching significance. His "To
the Sea,"† for example, is but thirty-one bars
long; yet within this limited frame he has confined a tone-picture which for breadth of conception and concentrated splendour of effect is
paralleled in the contemporary literature of the
piano only by himself. Consider, also, the
"Epilogue" in the revised version of the "Marionettes." The piece comprises only a score of

* The revised version, published in 1901, is referred to.
The original edition, which appeared in 1888, is decidedly
inferior.

† From the "Sea Pieces," for piano.

measures; yet within it the thought of the composer traverses a world of philosophical meditation: here is reflected the mood of one who looks with grave tenderness across the tragi-comedy of human life, in which, he would say to us, we are no less the playthings of a controlling destiny than are the figures of his puppet microcosm.

This scope and amplitude of expression are realised through a method at once plastic and unlaboured; his art has spontaneity — the deceptive spontaneity of the expert craftsman. It is not, in its elements, a strikingly novel style. His harmony, *per se*, is not unusual, if one sets it beside the surprising combinations evolved by such innovators as d'Indy, Debussy, and Strauss. It is in the novel disposition of familiar material — in what Mr. Apthorp has happily called his "free, instinctive application of the old in a new way" — that MacDowell's emphatic individuality consists. Whether it is a more signal achievement to create a new speech through the readjustment of established locutions than to evolve it from fresh and unworked elements, is open to debate. Be that as it may, however, MacDowell's achievement is of the former order.

His harmonic method is ingenious and pliable. An over-insistence upon certain formulas — eloquent enough in themselves — has been charged against it, and the accusation is not without foundation. MacDowell is exceedingly fond, for instance, of suspensions in the chord of the diminished seventh. There is scarcely a page throughout his later work in which one does not encounter this effect in but slightly varied form. Yet there is a continual richness in his harmonic texture. I can think of no other composer, save Wagner, whose chord-progressions are so full and opulent in colour. His tonal web is always densely woven — he avoids "thinness" as he avoids the banal phrase and the futile decoration. In addition to the plangency of his chord combinations, as such, his polyphonic skill is responsible for much of the solidity of his fabric. His pages, particularly in the more recent works, are studded with examples of felicitous and dexterous counterpoint — poetically significant, and of the most elastic and untrammelled contrivance. Even in passages of a merely episodic character, one is struck with the vitality and importance of his inner voices. Dissonance — in the sense in which we understand dissonance to-day — plays a comparatively unimportant part in his technical method. The climax of the second of the "Sea Pieces" — "From a Wandering Iceberg" — marks about as extreme a point of harmonic conflict as he ever touches. Nor has he been

profoundly affected by the passion for unbridled
chromaticism engendered in modern music by
the procedures of Chopin, Liszt, and Wagner.
Even in the earlier of the orchestral works,
"Hamlet and Ophelia" and "Lancelot and
Elaine"—both written in Germany in the days
when the genius of Wagner was an ambient and
inescapable flame—the writing is comparatively
free from chromatic effects.   On the other hand,
he is far less audaciously diatonic than Richard
Strauss.   His style is, in fact, a subtle blend of
opposing tendencies.

That his songs constitute almost a third of
the entire bulk of his work is not without significance; for his melodic gift is, probably, the
most notable possession of his art.   His insist-
ence upon the value and importance of the *melos*
was, indeed, one of his cardinal tenets; and he is,
in his practice, — whether writing for the voice,
for piano, or for orchestra, — inveterately and
frankly melodic: melodic with a suppleness, a
breadth, a freshness and spontaneity which are
anything but common in the typical music of our
day.   It is a curious experience to turn from the
music of such typical moderns as Loeffler and
Debussy, with its elusive melodic contours, its
continual avoidance of definite patterns, its passion for the esoteric and its horror of direct com-

munication, to the music of such a writer as
MacDowell. For he has accomplished the difficult and perilous feat of writing frankly without
obviousness, simply without triteness. His melodic outlines are firm, clean-cut, apprehendable;
but they are seldom commonplace in design.
His thematic substance at its best — in, say, the
greater part of the sonatas, the "Sea Pieces," the
"Woodland Sketches," the "Four Songs" of
op. 56 — has saliency, character, and often great
beauty; and even when it is not at its best — as
in much of his writing up to his opus 45 — it has
a spirit and colour that lift it securely above
mediocrity.

It must have already become evident to anyone who has followed this essay at an exposition
of MacDowell's art that his view of the traditional
musical forms is a liberal one. Which is briefly
to say that, although his application to his art
of the fundamental principles of musical design
is deliberate and satisfying, he shares the typical
modern distaste for the classic forms. His four
sonatas, his two piano concertos, and his two
"modern suites" for piano are his only important adventures in the traditional instrumental
moulds. The catalogue of his works is innocent
of any symphony, overture, string quartet, or
cantata. The major portion of his work is as

elastic and emancipated in form as it is uncon-
fined in spirit. He preferred to shape his inspiration upon the mould of a definite poetic
concept, rather than upon a constructive formula which was, for him, artificial and anomalous.
Even in his sonatas the classic prescription is
altered or abrogated at will in accordance with
the requirements of the underlying poetic idea.

CHAPTER IV

MacDowell's impulse toward significant expression was not slow in declaring itself. The first "modern suite" (op. 10), the earliest of his listed works, which at first glance seems to be merely a group of contrasted movements of innocently traditional aspect, with the expected Præludium, Presto, Intermezzo, Fugue, etc., contains, nevertheless, the germ of the programmatic principle; for at the head of the third movement (Andantino and Allegretto) one comes upon a motto from Virgil — "*Per amica silentia lunæ*," and the Rhapsodie is introduced with the

"*Lasciate ogni speranza, voi ch' entrate*"

of Dante. The Præludium of the second piano suite, op. 14, is also annotated, having been suggested by lines from Byron's "Manfred." In the "*Zwei Fantasiestücke*, op. 17 — "*Erzählung*" and "*Hexentanz*" — but more particularly in the "*Wald-Idyllen*" of op. 19 — "*Waldesstille*," "*Spiel der Nymphen*," "*Träumerei*," and "*Driadentanz*," — a definite poetic concept is implied.

114

Here the formative influence of Raff is evident.
The works which follow — "*Drei Poesien*"
("*Nachts am Meere*," "*Erzählung aus der Rit-
terzeit*," "*Ballade*"), and the "*Mondbilder*," after
Hans Christian Andersen — are of a similar
kind. The romanticism which pervades them is
not of a very finely distilled quality: they are not,
that is to say, the product of a clarified and wholly
personal vision — of the vision which prompted
the issue of such things as the "Woodland
Sketches," the "Sea Pieces," and the "New
England Idyls."   In these earlier works one feels
that the romantic view has been assumed somewhat vicariously — one can imagine the favourite
pupil of Raff producing a group of "*Wald-Idyllen*" quite as a matter of course, and without
interior conviction. Nor is the style marked by
individuality, except in occasional passages.
There are traces of his peculiar quality in the
first suite, — in the 6/8 passage of the Rhapsodie,
for example,—in portions of the first piano concerto (the *a piacere* passage toward the close of
the first movement is particularly characteristic),
in the *Erzählung*, and in No. 3 (*Traumerei*) of the
Wald-Idyllen; but the prevailing note of his style
at this time was, quite naturally, strongly Teutonic: one encounters in it the trail of Liszt, of
Schumann, of Raff, of Wagner.

Not until one reaches the "Hamlet and Ophelia" is it apparent that he is beginning to find himself. This work was written before he had completed his twenty-fourth year; yet the music is curiously ripe in feeling and accomplishment. There is breadth and steadiness of view in the conception, passion and sensitiveness in its embodiment. It is mellower, of a deeper and finer beauty, than anything he had previously done, though nowhere has it the inspiration of his later works.

The second piano concerto (op. 23), completed a year later, is fairly within the class of that order of music which it has been generally agreed to describe as "absolute." It is innocent of any programme, save for the fact that some of the ideas prompted by "Much Ado About Nothing," which were to form a "Beatrice and Benedick" symphonic poem, were, as I have related in a previous chapter, incorporated in the scherzo. Together with its companion work, the first piano concerto; the "Romanza" for 'cello and orchestra; the concert study, op. 36, and such conventional *morceaux* as the early "Serenata" and "Barcarolle" (of which, it should be noted, there are extremely few among his productions), it represents the very limited body of his writing which does not, in some degree, propose and enforce a definite poetic concept. Not elsewhere in his earlier work has MacDowell marshalled the materials of his art with so confident an artistry as he exhibits in this concerto. In substance the work is not extraordinary. The manner derives something from Grieg, more from Liszt, and there is comparatively little disclosure of personality. But the manipulation is, throughout, the work of a music-wright of brilliant executive capacity. In fundamental logic, in cohesion, flexibility, and symmetry of organism, it is a brilliantly successful accomplishment. As in all of MacDowell's writing, its allegiance is to the basic principles of structure and design, rather than to a traditional and arbitrary formula.

The succeeding opus (24), comprising the "Humoreske," "March," "Cradle Song," and "Czardas," is unimportant. Of the four pieces the gracious "Cradle Song" is of the most worth. The group as a whole belongs to that inconsiderable portion of his output which one cannot accept as of serious artistic consequence. With the "Lancelot and Elaine" (op. 25), however, one comes upon a work of the grade of the "Hamlet and Ophelia" music. MacDowell had a peculiar affinity for the spirit of the Arthurian tales, and he was happy in whatever musical transmutation of them he attempted. This tone-poem is, as he avows, "after Tennyson." The work follows consistently the larger action of the poem, and musical equivalents are sought and found for such crucial incidents as the meeting with Elaine, the tournament, Lancelot's downfall, his return to the court and the interview with Guinevere, the apparition of the funeral barge, and the soliloquy of Lancelot by the river bank. The work is dramatically conceived. There are passages of impressive tenderness, — as in the incident of the approaching barge; of climactic force, — as in the passage portraying the casting away of the trophies; and there are admirable details of workmanship. The scoring is full and adroit, though not very elaborate. As always with him, the instrumental texture is richly woven, although his utilisation of the possibilities of the orchestra is far from exhaustive. One misses, for example, the colouring of available harp effects, for which he appeared to have a distaste, since the instrument is not required in any of his orchestral works. That he was not satisfied with the scoring of the work is known. He remarked to Mr. Philip Hale that it was "too full of horns"; and in his own copy of the score, which I possess, he has made in pencil numerous changes in the instrumentation, much to its improvement; he has, for instance, in accord with his expressed feeling, reduced the prominence of the horns, allotting their parts, in certain important instances, to the wood-wind, trombones, or trumpets.

The "Six Idyls after Goethe," for piano (op. 28), are noteworthy as foreshadowing the candid impressionism which was to have its finest issue in the "Woodland Sketches," "Sea Pieces," and "New England Idyls." The Goethe paraphrases, although they have only a tithe of the graphic nearness and felicity of the later pieces, are yet fairly successful in their attempt to find a musical correspondence for certain definitely stated concepts and ideas — a partial fulfilment of the method implied in the earlier "*Wald-Idyllen*." He presents himself here as one who has yielded his imagination to an intimate contemplation of the natural world, and who already has, in some degree, the faculty of uttering whatever revelation of its loveliness or majesty has been vouchsafed. At once, in studying these pieces, one observes a wide departure in method and accomplishment from the style of the "*Wald-Idyllen*." In those, it seemed, the poet had somehow failed to compose "with his eye on the object": the vision lacked steadiness, lacked penetration — or it may be that the vision was

present, but not the power of notation. In the
Goethe paraphrases, on the other hand, we are
given, in a measure, the sense of the thing perceived; I say "in a measure," for his power of
acute and sympathetic observation and of eloquent transmutation had not yet come to its
highest pitch. Of the six "Idyls," three — "In
the Woods," "Siesta," and "To the Moonlight"
— are memorable, though uneven; and of these
the third, after Goethe's "An den Mond," adum-
brates faintly MacDowell's riper manner. The
"Silver Clouds," "Flute Idyl,"* and "Blue
Bell" are decidedly less characteristic.

His third orchestral work, the symphonic poem
"Lamia," is based upon the fantastic (and what
Mr. Howells would call unconscionably "romanticistic") poem of Keats. Begun during his
last year in Wiesbaden (1888), and completed
the following winter in Boston, it stands, in the
order of MacDowell's orchestral pieces, between
"Lancelot and Elaine" and the two "fragments"
after the "Song of Roland." On a fly-leaf of
the score MacDowell has written this glossary of
the story as told by Keats:

   "Lamia, an enchantress in the form of a serpent,

* The poems which suggested this and the preceding piece
were used again by MacDowell in two of the most admirable
of the "Eight Songs," op. 47.

loves Lycius, a young Corinthian. In order to win him she prays to Hermes, who answers her appeal by transforming her into a lovely maiden. Lycius meets her in the wood, is smitten with love for her, and goes with her to her enchanted palace, where the wedding is celebrated with great splendour. But suddenly Apollonius appears; he reveals the magic. Lamia again assumes the form of a serpent, the enchanted palace vanishes, and Lycius is found lifeless."

Now this is obviously just the sort of thing to stir the musical imagination of a young composer nourished on Liszt, Raff, and Wagner; and MacDowell (he was then in his twenty-seventh year) composed his tone-poem with evident gusto. Yet it is the weakest of his orchestral works — the weakest and the least characteristic. There is much Liszt in the score, and a good deal of Wagner. Only occasionally — as in the *pianissimo* passage for flutes, clarinets, and divided strings, following the first outburst of the full orchestra — does his own individuality emerge with any positiveness. MacDowell withheld the score from publication, at the time of its composition, because of his uncertainty as to its effect. He had not had an opportunity to secure a reading of it by one of the *Cur-Orchester* which had accommodatingly tried over his preceding scores at their rehearsals; and such a thing was of course out of the question in America. Not only was he reluctant to put it forth without such a test, but he lacked the funds to pay for its publication. He came to realise in later years, of course, that the music was immature and far from characteristic, though he still had a genuine affection for it. In a talk which I had with him a year before his collapse, he gave me the impression that he considered it at least as good a piece of work as its predecessors, "Hamlet and Ophelia" and "Lancelot and Elaine," though he made sport, in his characteristic way, of its occasional juvenility and its Wagneristic allegiances. He intended ultimately to revise and publish the score, and he allowed it to remain on the list of his works. After his death it was concluded that it would be wise to print the music, for several reasons. These were, first, because of the fear lest, if it were allowed to remain in manuscript, it might at some future time suffer from well-meant attempts at revision; and, secondly, because of the chance that it might be put forward, after the death of those who knew its history, in a way which would seem to make unwarranted pretensions for it, or would give rise to doubts as to its authenticity. In a word, it was felt that its immediate publication would obviate any possible misconception at some future time as to its true relation to MacDowell's artistic evolution. It was, therefore, published in October, 1908, twenty years after its composition, with a dedication to Mr. Henry T. Finck.

In "*Die Sarazenen*" and "*Die Schöne Aldâ,*" two "fragments" for orchestra after the "Song of Roland," numbered op. 30, a graver note is sounded. These "fragments," originally intended to form part of a "Roland" symphony, were published in 1891 in their present form, the plan for a symphony having been definitely abandoned. "*Die Sarazenen*" is a transcription of the scene in which Ganelon, the traitor in Charlemagne's camp through whose perfidy Roland met his death, swears to commit his crime. It is a forceful conception, barbaric in colour and rhythm, and picturesquely scored. The second fragment, "*Die Schöne Aldâ,*" is, however, a more memorable work, depicting the loveliness and the grieving of Aldâ, Roland's betrothed. In spite of its strong Wagnerian leanings, the music bears the impress of MacDowell's own style, and it has moments of rare loveliness. Both pieces are programmatic in bent, and, with excellent wisdom, MacDowell has quoted upon the fly-leaf of the score those portions of the "Song of Roland" from which the conception of the music sprang.

Like the "Idyls" after Goethe, the "Six

Poems" after Heine (op. 31), for piano, are devoted to the embodiment of a poetic subject, — with the difference that instead of the landscape impressionism of the Goethe studies we have a persistent impulse toward psychological suggestion. Each of the poems which he has selected for illustration has a burden of human emotion which the music reflects with varying success. The style is more individualised than in the Goethe pieces, and the invention is, on the whole, of a superior order. The "Scotch Poem" (No. 2) is the most successful of the set; the

> ". . . . . . *schöne, kranke Frau,*
> *Zartdurchsichtig und marmorblass,*"

and her desolate lamenting, are sharply projected, though scarcely with the power that he would have brought to bear upon the endeavour a decade later. Less effective, but more characteristic, is "The Shepherd Boy" (No. 5). This is almost, at moments, MacDowell in the happiest phase of his lighter vein. The transition from F minor to major, after the *fermata* on the second page, is as typical as it is delectable; and the fifteen bars that follow are of a markedly personal tinge. "From Long Ago" and "From a Fisherman's Hut" are less good, and "The Post Wagon" and "Monologue" are disappointing

— the latter especially so, because the exquisite poem which he has chosen to enforce, the matchless lyric beginning "*Der Tod, das ist die kühle Nacht,*" should, it seems, have offered an inspiring incentive.

In the "Four Little Poems" of op. 32 one encounters a piece which it is possible to admire without qualification: I mean the music conceived as an illustration to Tennyson's poem, "The Eagle." The three other numbers of this opus, "The Brook," "Moonshine," and "Winter," one can praise only in measured terms — although "Winter," which attempts a representation of the "widow bird" and frozen landscape of Shelley's lyric, has some measures that dwell persistently in the memory: but "The Eagle" is a superb achievement. Its deliberate purpose is to realise in tone the imagery and atmosphere of Tennyson's lines — an object which it accomplishes with triumphant completeness. As a feat of sheer tone-painting one recalls few things, of a similar scope and purpose, that surpass it in fitness, concision, and felicity. It displays a power of imaginative transmutation hitherto undisclosed in MacDowell's writing. Here are precisely the severe and lonely mood of the opening lines of the poem, the sense of inaccessible and wind-swept spaces, which Tennyson has so

magnificently and so succinctly conveyed. Here,
too, are the far-off, "wrinkled sea," and the final
cataclysmic and sudden descent: yet, despite the
literalism of the close, there is no yielding of
artistic sobriety in the result, for the music has
an unassailable dignity. It remains, even to-day,
one of MacDowell's most characteristic and
admirable performances.

Of the "Romance" for 'cello and orchestra
(op. 35), the Concert Study (op. 36), and "*Les
Orientales*" (op. 37), — three *morceaux* for piano,
after Victor Hugo, — there is no need to speak
in detail. "Perfunctory" is the word which one
must use to describe the creative impulse of which
they are the ungrateful legacy — an impulse less
spontaneous, there is reason to believe, than
utilitarian. Perhaps they may most justly be
characterised as almost the only instances in
which MacDowell gave heed to the possibility
of a reward not primarily and exclusively artistic.
They are sentimental and unleavened, and they
are far from worthy of his gifts, though they are
not without a certain rather inexpensive charm.

The "Marionettes" of op. 38 are in a wholly
different case. Published first in 1888, the year
of MacDowell's return to America, they were
afterward extensively revised, and now appear
under a radically different guise. In its present

form, the group comprises six *genre* studies —
"Soubrette," "Lover," "Witch," "Clown," "Villain," "Sweetheart" — besides two additions: a
"Prologue" and "Epilogue." Here MacDowell
is in one of his happiest moods. It was a fortunate and charming conceit which prompted the
plan of the series, with its half-playful, half-
ironic, yet lurkingly poetic suggestions; for in
spite of the mood of bantering gaiety which
placed the pieces in such mocking juxtaposition,
there is, throughout, an undertone of grave and
meditative tenderness which it is one of the
peculiar properties of MacDowell's art to
communicate and enforce. This is continually apparent in "The Lover" and "Sweetheart," fugi-
tively so in the "Prologue," and, in an irresistible
degree, in the exceedingly poetic and deeply felt
"Epilogue" — one of the most typical and beautiful of MacDowell's smaller works. The music
of these pieces is, as with other of his earlier works
that he has since revised, confusing to the
observer who attempts to place it among his productions in the order suggested by its opus number. For although in the list of his published
works the "Marionettes" follow immediately on
the heels of the Concert Study and "*Les Orientales*," the form in which they are now most
generally known represents the much later period

of the "Keltic" sonata — a fact which will, however, be sufficiently evident to anyone who studies the two versions carefully enough to perceive the difference between more or less experimental craftsmanship and ripe and heedful artistry. The observer will notice in these pieces, incidentally, the abandonment of the traditional Italian terms of expression and the substitution of English words and phrases, which are used freely and with adroitness to indicate every shade of the composer's meaning. In place of the stereotyped terms of the music-maker's familiarly limited vocabulary, we have such a system of direct and elastic expression as Schumann adopted. Thus one finds, in the "Prologue," such unmistakable and illuminating directions as: "with sturdy good humour," "pleadingly," "mockingly"; in the "Soubrette" — "coquettishly," "poutingly"; in the "Lover" — "questioningly"; in the "Villain"—"with sinister emphasis," "sardonically." This method, which MacDowell has followed consistently in all his later works, has obvious advantages; and it becomes in his hands a picturesque and stimulating means for the conveyance of his intentions. Its defect, equally obvious, is that it is not, like the conventional Italian terminology, universally intelligible.

The "Twelve Studies" of op. 39 are less original in conception and of less artistic moment than the "Marionettes." Their titles — among which are a "Hunting Song," a "Romance," a "Dance of the Gnomes," and others of like connotation — suggest, in a measure, that imperfectly realised romanticism which I have before endeavoured to separate from the intimate spirit of sincere romance which MacDowell has so often succeeded in embodying. The same thing is true, though in a less degree, of the suite for orchestra (op. 42). It is more Raff-like — not in effect but in conception — than anything he has done. There are four movements: "In a Haunted Forest," "Summer Idyl," "The Shepherdess' Song," and "Forest Spirits," together with a supplement, "In October," forming part of the original suite, but not published until several years later. The work, as a whole, has atmosphere, freshness, buoyancy, and it is scored with exquisite skill and charm; but somehow it does not seem either as poetic or as distinguished as one imagines it might have been made. It is carried through with delightful high spirits, and with an expert order of craftsmanship; but it lacks persuasion — lacks, to put it baldly, inspiration.

Passing over a sheaf of piano pieces, the

"Twelve Virtuoso Studies" of op. 46 (of which
the "Novelette" and "Improvisation" are most
noteworthy), we come to a stage of MacDowell's
development in which, for the first time, he presents himself as an assured and confident master
of musical impressionism and the possessor of a
matured and fully individualised style.

CHAPTER V

A MATURED IMPRESSIONIST

WITH the completion and production of his "Indian" suite for orchestra (op. 48) MacDowell came, in a measure, into his own. Mr. Philip Hale, writing apropos of a performance of the suite at a concert of the Boston Symphony Orchestra* in December, 1897, did not hesitate to describe the work as "one of the noblest compositions of modern times." Elsewhere he wrote concerning it: "The thoughts are the musical thoughts of high imagination; the expression is that of the sure and serene master. There are here no echoes of Raff, or Wagner, or Brahms, men that have each influenced mightily the musical thought of to-day. There is the voice of one composer: a virile, tender voice that does not stammer, does not break, does not wax hysterical: the voice of a composer that not only must pour out that which has accumulated within him, but

* The suite is dedicated to this Orchestra and its former conductor, Mr. Emil Paur.

131

knows all the resources of musical oratory — in a word, the voice of MacDowell."

MacDowell has derived the greater part of the thematic substance of the suite, as he acknowledges in a prefatory note, from melodies of the North American Indians, with the exception of a few subsidiary themes of his own invention. "If separate titles for the different movements are desired," he says in his note, "they should be arranged as follows: I. 'Legend'; II. 'Love Song'; III. 'In War-time'; IV. 'Dirge'; V. 'Village Festival'" — a concession in which again one traces a hint of the inexplicable and amusing reluctance of the musical impressionist to acknowledge without reservation the programmatic basis of his work. In the case of the "Indian" suite, however, the intention is clear enough, even without the proffered titles; for the several movements are unmistakably based upon firmly held concepts of a definite dramatic and emotional significance. As supplemental aids to the discovery of his poetic purposes, the phrases of direction which he has placed at the beginning of each movement are indicative, taken in connection with the titles which he sanctions. The first movement, "Legend," is headed: *Not fast. With much dignity and character;* the second movement, "Love Song," is to be played *Not fast. Ten-*

derly; the third movement, "In War-time," is marked: *With rough vigour, almost savagely;* the fourth, "Dirge": *Dirge-like, mournfully;* the fifth, "Village Festival": *Swift and light.*

Here, certainly, is food for the imagination, the frankest of invitations to the impressionable listener. There is no reason to believe that the music is built throughout upon such a detailed and specific plan as underlies, for example, the "Lancelot and Elaine"; the notable fact is that MacDowell has attained in this work to a power and weight of utterance, an eloquence of communication, a ripeness of style, and a security and strength of workmanship, which he had not hitherto brought to the fulfilment of an avowedly impressionistic scheme.* He has exposed the particular emotions and the essential character of his subject with deep sympathy and extraordinary imaginative force — at times with profoundly impressive effect, as in the first movement, "Legend," and the third, "In War-Time"; and in the overwhelmingly poignant "Dirge" he has achieved the most profoundly affecting threnody in music since the "Götterdämmerung" *Trauermarsch.* I am inclined to rank this

* The "Tragica" sonata, op. 45, which antedates the suite by several years, and of which I shall write in another chapter, has a considerably less definite content.

movement, with the sonatas and one or two of the "Woodland Sketches" and "Sea Pieces," as the choicest emanation of MacDowell's genius; and of these it is, I think, the most inspired and the most deeply felt. The extreme pathos of the opening section, with the wailing phrase in the muted strings under the reiterated G of the flutes (an inverted organ-point of sixteen *adagio* measures); the indescribable effect of the muted horn heard from behind the scenes, over an accompaniment of divided violas and 'cellos *con sordini;* the heart-shaking sadness and beauty of the succeeding passage for all the muted strings; the mysterious and solemn close: these are outstanding moments in a masterpiece of the first rank: a page which would honour any music-maker, living or dead.

In the suite as a whole he has caught and embodied the fundamental spirit of his theme: these are the sorrows and laments and rejoicings, not of our own day and people, but of the vanished life of an elemental and dying race; here is the solitude of dark forests, of illimitable and lonely prairies, and the sombreness and wildness of one knows not what grim tragedies and romances and festivities enacted in the shadow of a fading past.

Into the discussion of the relation between such works as the "Indian" suite and the establishment of a possible "American" school of music I shall not intrude. To those of us who believe that such a "school," whether desirable or not, can never be created through conscious effort, and who are entirely willing to permit time and circumstance to bring about its establishment, the subject is as wearisome as it is unprofitable. The logic of the belief that it is possible to achieve a representative nationalism in music by the ingenuous process of adopting the idiom of an alien though neighbouring race is not immediately apparent; and although MacDowell in this suite has admittedly derived his basic material from the North American aborigines, he never, so far as I am aware, claimed that his impressive and noble score constitutes, for that reason, a representatively national utterance. He perceived, doubtless, that territorial propinquity is quite a different thing from racial affinity; and that a musical art derived from either Indian or Ethiopian sources can be "American" only in a partial and quite unimportant sense. He recognised, and he affirmed the belief, that racial elements are transitory and mutable, and that provinciality in art, even when it is called patriotism, makes for a probable oblivion.

I have already dwelt upon MacDowell's preoccupation with the pageant of the natural world.

If one is tempted, at times, to praise in him the celebrant of the "mystery and the majesty of earth" somewhat at the expense of the musical humanist, it is because he has in an uncommon degree the intimate visualising faculty of the essential Celt. "In all my work," he avowed a few years before his death, "there is the Celtic influence. I love its colour and meaning. The development in music of that influence is, I believe, a new field." That it was a note which he was pre-eminently qualified to strike and sustain is beyond doubt: and, as he seems to have realised, he had the field to himself. He is, strangely enough, the first Celtic influence of genuine vitality and importance which has been exerted upon creative music — a singular but incontestable fact. As it is exerted by him it has an exquisite authenticity. Again and again one is aware that the "sheer, inimitable Celtic note," which we have long known how to recognise in another art, is being sounded in the music of this composer who has in his heart and brain so much of "the wisdom of old romance." With him one realises that "natural magic" is, as Mr. Yeats has somewhere said, "but the ancient worship of Nature and that troubled ecstasy before her, that certainty of all beautiful places being haunted, which is brought into men's minds." We have

observed the operation of this impulse in such
comparatively immature productions as the
"*Wald-Idyllen*" and the "Idyls" after Goethe,
in the "Four Little Poems" of op. 32, and in
the first orchestral suite; but it is in the much
later "Woodland Sketches" and "Sea Pieces,"
for piano, that the tendency comes to its finest
issue.

Music, of course — from Frohberger and
Haydn to Mendelssohn, Wagner, Raff, and Debussy — abounds in examples of natural imagery. In claiming a certain excellence for his
method one need scarcely imply that MacDowell
has ever threatened the supremacy of such things
as the "Rheingold" prelude or the "Walküre"
fire music. It is as much by reason of his choice
of subjects as because of the peculiar vividness
and felicity of his expression, that he occupies so
single a place among tone-poets of the external
world. He has never attempted such vast frescoes as Wagner delighted to paint. Of his descriptive music by far the greater part is written
for the piano; so that, at the start, a very definite
limitation is imposed upon magnitude of plan.
You cannot suggest on the piano, with any ade-
quacy of effect, a mountain-side in flames, or the
prismatic arch of a rainbow, or the towering
architecture of cloud forms; so MacDowell has

confined himself within the bounds of such can-
vases as he paints upon in his "Four Little
Poems" ("The Eagle," "The Brook," "Moonshine," "Winter"), in his first orchestral suite,
and in the inimitable "Woodland Sketches" and
"Sea Pieces." Thus his themes are starlight, a
water-lily, will o' the wisps, a deserted farm, a
wild rose, the sea-spell, deep woods, an old garden. As a fair exemplification of his practice,
consider, let me say, his "To a Water-lily," from
the "Woodland Sketches." It is difficult to
recall anything in objective tone-painting, for
the piano or for the orchestra, conceived and
executed quite in the manner of this remarkable
piece of lyrical impressionism. Of all the composers who have essayed tonal transcriptions of
the phases of the outer world, I know of none
who has achieved such vividness and suggestive-
ness of effect with a similar condensation. The
form is small; but these pieces are no more justly
to be dismissed as mere "miniature work" than
is Wordsworth's "Daffodils," which they parallel
in delicacy of perception, intensity of vision, and
perfection of accomplishment. The question of
bulk, length, size, has quite as much pertinence
in one case as in the other. In his work in this
sort, MacDowell is often as one who, having
fallen, through the ignominies of daily life,

among the barren makeshifts of reality, "remembers the enchanted valleys." It is touched at times with the deep and wistful tenderness, the primæval nostalgia, which is never very distant from the mood of his writing, and in which, again, one is tempted to trace the essential Celt. It is this close kinship with the secret presences of the natural world, this intimate responsiveness to elemental moods, this quick sensitiveness to the aroma and the magic of places, that sets him recognisably apart.

If in the "Indian" suite MacDowell disclosed the full maturity of his powers of imaginative and structural design, it is in the "Woodland Sketches" (op. 51) that his speech, freed from such incumbrances as were imposed upon it by his deliberate adoption of an exotic idiom, assumes for the first time some of its most engaging and distinctive characteristics. Consider, for example, number eight of the group, "A Deserted Farm." Here is the quintessence of his style in one of its most frequent aspects. The manner has a curious simplicity, yet it would be difficult to say in what, precisely, the simplicity consists; it has striking individuality, — yet the particular trait in which it resides is not easily determined. The simplicity is certainly not of the harmonic plan, nor of the melodic outline, which are subtly yet frankly conceived; and the individuality does not lie in any eccentricity or determined novelty of effect. Both the flavour of simplicity and of personality are, one concludes, more a spiritual than an anatomical possession of the music. Its quality is as intangible and pervasive as that dim magic of "unremembering remembrance" that is awakened in some by the troubling tides of spring; it is apparently as unsought for as are the naïve utterances of folk-song. It is his unfailing charm, and it is everywhere manifest in his later work: that spontaneity and *insouciance*, that utter absence of self-consciousness, which is in nothing so surprising as in its serene antithesis to what one has come to accept — too readily, it may be — as the dominant accent of musical modernity.

These pieces have an inescapable fragrance, tenderness, and zest. "To a Wild Rose," "Will o' the Wisp," "In Autumn," "From Uncle Remus," and "By a Meadow Brook" are slight in poetic substance, though executed with charm and humour; but the five other pieces — "At an Old Trysting Place," "From an Indian Lodge," "To a Water-lily," "A Deserted Farm," and "Told at Sunset" — are of a different calibre. With the exception of "To a Water-lily," whose quality is uncomplex and unconcealed, these tone-poems in little are a curious blend of what, lacking an apter name, one must call nature-poetry, and psychological suggestion; and they are remarkable for the manner in which they focus great richness of emotion into limited space. "At an Old Trysting Place," "From an Indian Lodge," "A Deserted Farm," and "Told at Sunset," imply a consecutive dramatic purpose which is emphasised by their connection through a hint of thematic community. The element of drama, though, is not insisted upon — indeed, a large portion of the searching charm of these pieces lies in their tactful reticence.

In the "Sea Pieces" of op. 55 a larger impulse is at work. The set comprises eight short pieces, few of them over two pages in length; yet they are modelled upon ample lines, and they have, in a conspicuous degree, that property to which I have alluded — the property of suggesting within a limited framework an emotional or dramatic content of large and far-reaching significance. I spoke in an earlier chapter, in this connection, of the first of these pieces, "To the Sea." I must repeat that this tone-poem seems to me one of the most entirely admirable things in the literature of the piano; and it is typical, in the main, of the volume. MacDowell is one of the comparatively few composers who have been thrall

to the spell of the sea; none, I think, has felt
that spell more irresistibly or has communicated
it with more conquering an eloquence. This
music is full of the glamour, the awe, the mystery,
of the sea; of its sinister and terrible beauty, but
also of its tonic charm, its secret allurement.
Here is sea poetry to match with that of Whitman and Swinburne. The music is drenched in
salt-spray, wind-swept, exhilarating. There are
pages in it through which rings the thunderous
laughter of the sea in its mood of cosmic and
terrifying elation, and there are pages through
which drift sun-painted mists — mists that both
conceal and disclose enchanted vistas and appari-
tions. There is an exhilaration even in his
titles (which he has supplemented with mottos):
as "To the Sea," "From a Wandering Iceberg,"
"Starlight," "From the Depths," "In Mid-
Ocean." I make no concealment of my unqualified admiration for these pieces: with the sonatas,
the "Dirge" from the "Indian" suite, and certain of the "Woodland Sketches," they record, I
think, his high-water mark. He has carried
them through with superb gusto, with unweary-
ing imaginative fervour. In "To the Sea,"
"From the Depths," and "In Mid-Ocean," it is
the sea of Whitman's magnificent apostrophe
that he celebrates — the sea of

> "brooding scowl and murk,"

of

> "unloosed hurricanes,"

speaking, imperiously,

> "with husky-haughty lips";

while elsewhere, as in the "Wandering Iceberg" and "Nautilus" studies, the pervading tone is of Swinburne's

> "deep divine dark dayshine of the sea."

"Starlight" is of a brooding and solemn tenderness. The "Song" and "A.D. MDCXX." (a memoir of the notorious galleon of the Pilgrims) are in a lighter vein. The tonal plangency, the epic quality, of these studies is extraordinary, — exposing a tendency toward an orchestral fulness and breadth of style that will offer a more pertinent theme for comment in a consideration of the sonatas. Their littleness is wholly a quantitative matter; their spiritual and imaginative substance is not only of rare quality, but of striking amplitude.

We come now to the final volumes in the series of what one may as well call pianistic "nature-studies": the "Fireside Tales" (op. 61) and "New England Idyls" (op. 62), which, together with the songs of op. 60, constitute the

last of his published works (they were all issued
in 1902). In these last piano pieces there is
a new quality, an unaccustomed accent.   One
notes it on the first page of the opening number of the "Fireside Tales," "An Old Love
Story," where the voice of the composer seems to
have taken on an unfamiliar *timbre*.   There is
here a turn of phrase, a quality of sentiment,
which are notably fresh and strange.   There is
in this, and in "By Smouldering Embers," a
graver tenderness, a more pervasive sobriety,
than he had revealed before.   Read over the
D-flat major section of "An Old Love Story."
Throughout MacDowell's previous work one will
find no passage quite like it in contour and emotion.   It is quieter, more ripely poised, than
anything in his earlier manner that I can recall.
"Of Br'er Rabbit," "From a German Forest,"
"Of Salamanders," and "A Haunted House,"
are in his familiar vein; but again the new note
is sounded in the concluding number of the book,
"By Smouldering Embers."

In the "New England Idyls," the point is still
more evident.   One passes over "From an Old
Garden" and "Midsummer" as belonging funda-
mentally to the period of the "Woodland
Sketches" and "Sea Pieces."   But one halts at
"Mid-Winter," No. 3 of the collection; with those

The "house of dreams untold" — the log cabin in the woods at Peterboro where MacDowell composed, and where most of his later music was written

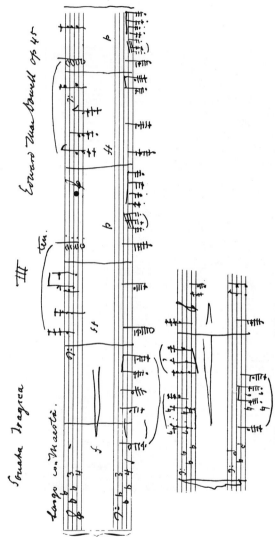

FACSIMILE OF A PORTION OF THE MS. OF THE "SONATA TRAGICA"

fifteen bars in E-flat major in the middle section, one enters upon unfamiliar ground in the various and delectable region of MacDowell's fantasy. So in the succeeding piece, "With Sweet Lavender": he had not given us in any of his former writing a theme similar in quality to the one with which he begins the thirteenth bar. "In Deep Woods" is less unusual — is, in fact, strongly suggestive, in harmonic colour, of the shining sonorities of the "Wandering Iceberg" study in the "Sea Pieces." The "Indian Idyl," "To an Old White Pine," and "From Puritan Days" are also contrived in the familiar idiom of the earlier volumes, though they are unfailingly resourceful in invention and imaginative vigour. In "From a Log Cabin," though, we come upon as surprising a thing as MacDowell's art had yielded us since the appearance of the "Woodland Sketches." I doubt if, in the entire body of his writing, one will find a lovelier, a more intimate utterance. It bears as a motto the words — strangely prophetic when he wrote them — which are now inscribed on the memorial tablet near his grave: —

> "A house of dreams untold,
> It looks out over the whispering tree-tops
> And faces the setting sun."

The music of this piece is suffused with a mood

that is Schumann-like in its intense sincerity of impulse, yet with a passionate fulness and ardour not elsewhere to be paralleled. It is steeped in an atmosphere which is felt in no other of his works, is the issue of an inspiration more profoundly contemplative than any to which he had hitherto responded.

CHAPTER VI

THE SONATAS

MacDowell never hesitated, as I have elsewhere said, to adapt — some would say "warp"
— the sonata form to the needs of his poetic
purposes. Moreover, he declared his convictions as to the considerations which should govern
its employment. "If the composer's ideas do
not imperatively demand treatment in that [the
sonata] form," he has observed — "that is, if his
first theme is not actually dependent upon his
second and side themes for its poetic fulfilment
— he has not composed a sonata movement, but a
potpourri, which the form only aggravates."
There can be little question of the success which
has attended his application of this principle to
his own performances in this field, nor of the
skill and tact with which he has reshaped the
form in accordance with his chosen poetic or
dramatic scheme.

His four sonatas belong undeniably, though
with a variously strict allegiance, to the domain
of programme-music. Neither the "Tragica,"

the "Eroica," the "Norse," nor the "Keltic,"
makes its appeal exclusively to the tonal sense.
If one looks to these works for the particular
kind of gratification which he is accustomed to
derive, for example, from a sonata by Brahms
(to name the most extreme of contrasts), he will
not find it.   It is impossible fully to appreciate
and enjoy the last page of the "Keltic," for instance, without some knowledge of the dramatic
crisis upon which the musician has built — although its beauty and power, as sheer music, are
immediately perceptible.

With the exception of the "Tragica," the
poetic substratum of the sonatas has been avowed
with more or less particularity.   In the "Tragica"
— his first essay in the form — he has vouchsafed only the general indication of his purpose
which is declared in the title of the work, though
it is known that in composing the music Mac-
Dowell was moved by the memory of his grief
over the death of his master Raff (it might stand
even more appropriately as a commentary on
the tragedy of his own life).   The tragic note is
sounded, with impressive authority and force, in
the brief introduction, *largo maestoso*.   The
music, from the first, drives to the very heart of
the subject: there is neither pose nor bombast in
the presentation of the thought; and this attitude

is maintained throughout — in the ingratiating loveliness of the second subject, in the fierce striving of the middle section, in the noble and sombre slow movement, — a *largo* of profound pathos and dignity, — and in the dramatic and impassioned close (the scherzo is, I think, less good). Of this final *allegro* an exposition has been vouchsafed. While in the preceding movements, it is said, he aimed at expressing tragic details, in the last he has tried to generalise. He wished "to heighten the darkness of tragedy by making it follow closely on the heels of triumph. Therefore, he attempted to make the last movement a steadily progressive triumph, which, at its close, is utterly broken and shattered, thinking that the most poignant tragedy is that of catastrophe in the hour of triumph. . . . In doing this he has tried to epitomise the whole work." The meaning of the *coda* is thus made clear: a climax approached with the utmost pomp and brilliancy, and cut short by a *precipitato* descent in octaves, *fff*, ending with a reminiscence of the portentous subject of the introduction. It is a profoundly moving conclusion to a noble work — a work which Mr. James Huneker has not extravagantly called "the most marked contribution to solo sonata literature since Brahms' F-minor piano sonata"; yet it is not so fine a work as any one

of the three sonatas which MacDowell afterward
wrote. The style evinces, for the first time in
his piano music, the striking orchestral character
of his thought — yet the writing is not, para-
doxical as it may seem, unpianistic. The suggestion of orchestral relationships is contained
in the massiveness of the harmonic texture,
and in the cumulative effect of the climaxes
and crescendi. He conveys an impression of
extended tone-spaces, of a largeness, complexity, and solidity of structure, which are
peculiar to his own music, and which presup-
pose a rather disdainful view of the limitations of mere strings and hammers; yet it is all
playable: its demands are formidable, but not
prohibitive.

In 1895 MacDowell published his "Sonata
Eroica" (op. 50), and those who had wondered
how he could better his performance in the
"Tragica" received a fresh demonstration of the
extent of his gifts. For these sonatas of his constitute an ascending series, steadily progressive in
excellence of substance and workmanship. They
are, on the whole, I think it will be determined,
his most significant and important contribution
to musical art. The "Eroica" bears the motto,
"*Flos regum Arthuris,*" and as a further index
to its content MacDowell has given this explana-

tion: "While not exactly programme music,"*
he says, "I had in mind the Arthurian legend
when writing this work. The first movement
typifies the coming of Arthur. The scherzo was
suggested by a picture of Doré showing a knight
in the woods surrounded by elves. The third
movement was suggested by my idea of Guinevere. That following represents the passing of
Arthur." MacDowell had intended to inscribe
the scherzo: "After Doré"; but he finally thought
better of this because, as he told Mr. N. J.
Corey, "the superscription seemed to single it
out too much from the other movements." Concerning this movement Mr. Corey writes: "The
passage which it [the Doré picture] illustrates,
may be found in [Tennyson's] *Guinevere*, in the
story of the little novice, following a few lines
after the well known 'Late, late, so late!' poem.
I always had a little feeling," continues Mr.
Corey, "that the sonata would have been stronger,
from a programme standpoint, with this movement omitted — that it had perhaps been included largely as a concession to the traditions

* It must be confessed that this qualification is a little
difficult to grasp. Is not the sonata dependent for its complete understanding upon a knowledge of its literary basis?
MacDowell exhibits here the half-heartedness which I have
elsewhere remarked in his attitude toward representative
music.

of sonata form. The fact that no scherzos were included in the two sonatas that followed, strengthened my opinion in regard to this. I questioned him in regard to it later when I saw him in New York, and he replied that it was a matter over which he had pondered considerably, and one which had influenced him in the composition of the last two sonatas, as the insertion of a scherzo in such a scheme did seem something like an interruption, or 'aside.'"

In this sonata MacDowell has been not only faithful to his text, he has illuminated it. Indeed, I think it would not be extravagant to say that he has given us here the noblest musical incarnation of the Arthurian legend which we have. It is singular, by the way, how frequently one is impelled to use the epithet "noble" in praising MacDowell's work; in reference to the "Sonata Eroica" it has an emphatic aptness, for nobility is the keynote of this music. If the work, as a whole, has not the dynamic power of the "Tragica," the weight and gravity of substance, it is both a lovelier and a more lovable work, and it is everywhere more significantly accented. He has written few things more luxuriantly beautiful than the "Guinevere" movement, nothing more elevated and ecstatic than the apotheosis which ends the work. The diction throughout is richer

and more variously contrasted than in the earlier
work, and his manipulation of the form is more
elastic.

Apparent as is the advance of the "Eroica"
over its predecessor, the difference between these
and the two later sonatas — the "Norse" and
the "Keltic" — is even more marked. The first
of these, the "Norse" sonata (op. 57) appeared
five years after the publication of the "Eroica."
In the interval he had put forth the "Woodland
Sketches," the "Sea Pieces," and the songs of
op. 56 and op. 58; and he had, evidently, exam-
ined deeply into the resources and potentialities
of his art. He had hitherto done nothing quite
like these two later sonatas; they are based upon
larger and more intricate plans than their predecessors, are more determined and confident in
their expression of personality, riper in style and
far freer in form: they are, in fact, MacDowell
at his most salient and distinguished. He has
placed these lines of his own on the first page
of the score of the "Norse" (which is dedicated
to Grieg) :

> "Night had fallen on a day of deeds.
> The great rafters in the red-ribbed hall
> Flashed crimson in the fitful flame
> Of smouldering logs;
> And from the stealthy shadows

That crept 'round Harald's throne
Rang out a Skald's strong voice
With tales of battles won:
Of Gudrun's love
And Sigurd, Siegmund's son."

Here, evidently, is a subject after his own heart,
presenting such opportunities as he is at his happiest in improving — and he has improved them
magnificently. The spaciousness of the plan,
the boldness of the drawing, the fulness and
intensity of the colour scheme, engage one's
attention at the start. He has indulged almost
to its extreme limits his predilection for extended
chord formations and for phrases of heroic span
— as in, for example, almost the whole of the
first movement. The pervading quality of the
musical thought is of a resistless and passionate
virility. It is steeped in the barbaric and splendid
atmosphere of the sagas. There are pages of
epical breadth and power, passages of elemental
vigour and ferocity — passages, again, of an
exquisite tenderness and poignancy. Of the
three movements which the work comprises, the
first makes the most lasting impression, although
the second (the slow movement) has a haunting
subject, which is recalled episodically in the final
movement in a passage of unforgettable beauty
and character.

With the publication, in 1901, of the "Keltic" sonata (his fourth, op. 59),* MacDowell achieved a conclusive demonstration of his capacity as a creative musician of unquestionable importance. Not before had he given so convincing an earnest of the larger aspect of his genius: neither in the three earlier sonatas, in the "Sea Pieces," nor in the "Indian" suite, had he attained an equal magnitude, an equal scope and significance. Nowhere else in his work are the distinguishing traits of his genius so strikingly disclosed — the breadth and reach of imagination, the magnetic vitality, the richness and fervour, the conquering poetic charm. Here you will find a beauty which is as "the beauty of the men that take up spears and die for a name," no less than "the beauty of the poets that take up harp and sorrow and the wandering road" — a harp shaken with a wild and piercing music, a sorrow that is not of to-day, but of a past when dreams were actual and imperishable, and men lived the tales of beauty and of wonder which now are but a discredited and fading memory.

It was a fortunate, if not an inevitable, event, in view of his temperamental affiliations with the Celtic genius, that MacDowell should have been made aware of the suitability for musical treat-

* Dedicated, like the "Norse," to Grieg.

ment of the ancient heroic chronicles of the Gaels, and that he should have gone for his inspiration, in particular, to the legends comprised in the famous Cycle of the Red Branch: that wonderful group of epics which comprises, among other tales, the story of the matchless Deirdré, —whose loveliness was such, so say the chroniclers, that "not upon the ridge of earth was there a woman so beautiful," — and the life and adventures and glorious death of the incomparable Cuchullin. These two kindred legends MacDowell has welded into a coherent and satisfying whole; and in a verse with which he prefixes the sonata, he gives this index to its poetic content:

> "Who minds now Keltic tales of yore,
>   Dark Druid rhymes that thrall;
>   Deirdré's song, and wizard lore
>   Of great Cuchullin's fall."

At the time of the publication of the sonata he wrote to me as follows concerning it:

". . . Here is the sonata, which it is a pleasure to me to offer you as a token of sympathy. I enclose also some lines [of his own verse] anent Cuchullin, which, however, do not entirely fit the music, and which I hope to use in another musical form. They may serve, however, to aid the understanding of the *stimmung* of the sonata. Cuchullin's story is in touch with the Deirdré-Naesi tale; and, as with my 3rd Sonata, the music is more a commentary on the subject than an actual depiction of it."

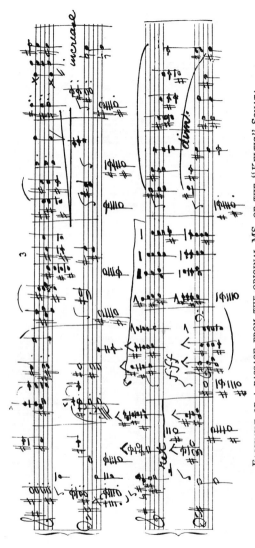

Facsimile of a passage from the original MS. of the "Keltic" Sonata

THE MUSIC-ROOM AT PETERBORO

The "lines anent Cuchullin" I quote below. They do not, as he said, have a parallel in the sonata as a whole; but in the *coda* of the last movement (of which I shall speak later) he has attempted a commentary on the scene which he here describes:

"Cuchullin fought and fought in vain,
   'Gainst faery folk and Druid thrall:
And as the queenly sun swept down,
In royal robes, red gold besown,
With one last lingering glance
He sate himself in lonely state
Against a giant monolith,
To wait Death's wooing call.
None dared approach the silent shape
That froze to iron majesty,
Save the wan, mad daughters of old Night,
Blind, wandering maidens of the mist,
Whose creeping fingers, cold and white,
Oft by the sluggard dead are kissed.
And yet the monstrous Thing held sway,
No living soul dared say it nay;
When lo! upon its shoulder still,
Unconscious of its potent will,
There perched a preening birdling gray,
A'weary of the dying day;
And all the watchers knew the lore:
Cuchullin was no more."

To Mr. Corey MacDowell wrote:

". . . Even though you are not on intimate terms with Deirdré, Cuchullin, etc., you will easily perceive from the music that something extremely unpleasant is happening. Joking aside, I will confess to a certain fascination the subject has for me. So much so that my 'motto' [the original motto — the verses which I have quoted above] spread beyond the music; therefore I am going to make a different work of the former, and for the sonata I adopted the modest quatrain that is printed in it. . . . Like the third, this fourth sonata is more of a 'bardic' rhapsody on the subject than an attempt at actual presentation of it, although I have made use of all the suggestion of tone-painting in my power, — just as the bard would have reinforced *his* speech with gesture and facial expression."

He aimed to make his music, as he says, "more a commentary on the subject than an actual depiction of it"; but the case would be stated more truly, I think, if one were to say that he has penetrated to the heart of the entire body of legends, has imbued himself with their ultimate spirit and significance, and has bodied it forth in his music with splendid veracity and eloquence. He has attempted no mere musical recounting of those romances of the ancient Gaelic world at which he hints in his brief motto. It would be juster to say, rather, that he has recalled in his music the very life and presence of the Gaelic prime — that he has "unbound the Island harp." Above all, he has achieved that "heroic beauty" which, believes Mr. Yeats, has been fading out of the arts since "that decadence we call progress set voluptuous beauty in its place" — that heroic beauty which is of the very essence of the imaginative life of the primitive Celts, and which the Celtic "revival" in contemporary letters has so signally failed to revive. For it is, I repeat, the heroic Gaelic world that MacDowell has made to live again in his music: that miraculous world of stupendous passions and aspirations, of bards and heroes and great adventure — the world of Cuchullin the Unconquerable, and Laeg, and Queen Meave; of Naesi, and Deirdré the Beautiful, and Fergus, and Connla the Harper, and those kindred figures, lovely or greatly tragical, that are like no other figures in the world's mythologies.

This sonata marks the consummation of his evolution toward the acme of powerful expression. It is cast in a mould essentially heroic; it has its moods of tenderness, of insistent sweetness, but these are incidental: the governing mood is signified in the tremendous exordium with which the work opens, and which is sustained, with few deviations, throughout the work. Deirdré he has realised exquisitely in his middle movement: that is her image, in all its fragrant loveliness. MacDowell has limned her musically in a manner worthy of comparison with the sumptuous pen-portrait of her in Standish

O'Grady's "Cuculain": "a woman of wondrous beauty, bright gold her hair, eyes piercing and splendid, tongue full of sweet sounds, her countenance like the colour of snow blended with crimson."

In the close of the last movement we are justified in seeing a translation of the sublime tradition of Cuchullin's death. This it is which furnished MacDowell with the theme that he celebrates in the lines of verse which I have quoted above. I believe that he was planning an orchestral setting of this scene; and that, had he lived, we should have had from him a symphonic poem, "Cuchullin."

The manner of the hero's death is thus described by Standish O'Grady: "Cuculain sprang forth, but as he sprang, Lewy MacConroi pierced him through the bowels. Then fell the great hero of the Gael. Thereat the sun darkened, and the earth trembled . . . when, with a crash, fell that pillar of heroism, and that flame of the warlike valour of Erin was extinguished. . . . Then Cuculain, raising his eyes, saw thence northwards from the lake a tall pillar-stone, the grave of a warrior slain there in some ancient war. With difficulty he reached it and he leaned awhile against the pillar, for his mind wandered, and he knew nothing for a space. After that he took off his brooch, and removing the torn bratta [girdle], he passed it round the top of the pillar, where there was an indentation in the stone, and passed the ends under his arms and around his breast, tying with languid hands a loose knot, which soon was made fast by the weight of the dying hero; thus they beheld him standing with the drawn sword in his hand, and the rays of the setting sun bright on his panic-striking helmet. So stood Cuculain, even in death-pangs, a terror to his enemies, for a deep spring of stern valour was opened in his soul, and the might of his unfathomable spirit sustained him. Thus perished Cuculain . . ."

Superb as this is, it is paralleled by Mac-Dowell's tone-picture. That, for nobility of conception, for majestic solemnity and pathos, is a musical performance which measures up to the level of superlative achievements.

If there is anything in the literature of the piano since the death of Beethoven which, for combined passion, dignity, breadth of style, weight of momentum, and irresistible plangency of emotion, is comparable to the four sonatas which have been considered here, I do not know of it. And I write these words with a perfectly definite consciousness of all that they may be held to imply.

CHAPTER VII

THE SONGS

ANY one who should undertake casually to examine MacDowell's songs *seriatim*, beginning with his earliest listed work in this form — the "Two Old Songs," op. 9 — would not improbably be struck by an apparent lack of continuity and logic in the initial stages of his artistic development. At first glance, MacDowell seems to have attained a phenomenal ripeness and individuality of expression in these songs, which head the catalogue of his published works; whereas the songs of the following opus (11–12) are conventional and unimportant. The explanation, which I have elsewhere intimated, is simple. The songs of op. 11 and 12, issued in 1883, were the first of his *Lieder* to appear in print; the songs numbered op. 9, which would appear to antedate them in composition and publication, were not written until a decade later, when they were issued under an arbitrary opus number as a matter of expediency. Their proper place in MacDowell's musical history is, therefore, about synchronous with the mature and characteristic "Eight Songs" of op. 47. From the five songs now published in one volume as op. 11 and 12, the progress of MacDowell's art as a song writer is both steady and intelligible.

He has not been especially prolific in this field, when one thinks of Grieg's one hundred and twenty songs, and of Brahms' one hundred and ninety-six; not to mention Schumann's two hundred and forty-eight, or Schubert's amazing six hundred and over. MacDowell has written forty-two songs for single voice and piano, together with a number of ingenious and effective pieces for men's voices and for mixed chorus.

He has avowed his methods and principles as a song writer. In an interview published a few years before his death he declared his opinion to be that "song writing should follow declamation" — that the composer "should declaim the poems in sounds: the attention of the hearer should be fixed upon the central point of declamation. The accompaniment should be merely a background for the words. Harmony is a frightful den for the small composer to get into — it leads him into frightful nonsense. Too often the accompaniment of a song becomes a piano fantasie with no resemblance to the melody. Colour and harmony under such conditions mislead the composer; he uses it instead of the line which he at the moment is setting, and obscures the central point, the words, by richness of tissue and overdressing; and all modern music is labouring under that. He does not seem to pause to think that music was not made merely for pleasure, but to say things.

"Language and music have nothing in common. In one way, that which is melodious in verse becomes doggerel in music, and meter is hardly of value. Sonnets in music become abominable. I have made many experiments for finding the affinity of language and music. The two things are diametrically opposed, unless music is free to distort syllables. A poem may be of only four words, and yet those four words may contain enough suggestion for four pages of music; but to found a song on those four words would be impossible. For this reason the paramount value of the poem is that of its suggestion in the field of instrumental music, where a single line may be elaborated upon. . . . To me, in this respect, the poem holds its highest value of suggestion. . . . A short poem would take a lifetime to express; to do it in as many bars of music is impossible. The words clash with the music, they fail to carry the full suggestion of the poem. . .

"Many poems contain syllables ending with

e or other letters not good to sing.   Some excep-
tionally beautiful poems possess this shortcoming,
and, again, words that prove insurmountable
obstacles.   I have in mind one by Aldrich in
which the word 'nostrils' occurs in the very first
verse, and one cannot do anything with it.   Much
of the finest poetry — for instance, the wonderful
writings of Whitman — proves unsuitable, yet it
has been undertaken. . . .

"A song, if at all dramatic, should have climax,
form, and plot, as does a play.   Words to me
seem so paramount and, as it were, apart in
value from the musical setting, that, while I
cannot recall the melodies of many of the songs
that I have written, the words of them are so
indelibly impressed upon my mind that they are
very easy of recall. . . . Music and poetry cannot
be accurately stated unless one has written both."

It is clear that these are the views of a composer
who placed veracious declamation of the poetic
idea very much to the front in his conception of
the art of the song-writer.   They explain in
part, also, the fact that MacDowell himself wrote
the words of many of his songs, though, quite
characteristically, he did not avow the fact in the
printed music.   The verses of all the songs of
op. 56, save one, op. 58, and op. 60 (the last three
sets that he wrote), of the "Slumber Song" of

op. 9, of "The Robin Sings in the Apple Tree,"
"Confidence," and "The West Wind Croons in
the Cedar Trees" (op. 47), and of some of the
choruses, were of his authorship. He enjoyed
what he called "stringing words together," and
most of his verses were written off-hand, with a
facility which betrayed the marked gift for verbal
expression which is apparent in his often admi-
rably stated lectures. But his especial reason for
writing the words for his songs was his difficulty
in finding texts which quite suited him. Many
poems which he would have liked to set were, as
he explained in the words I have quoted, full of
snags in the way of unsingable words. And
though it used to make him uncomfortable to do
so, he often felt compelled for this reason to refuse
much otherwise excellent poetry that was sent
to him with the request that he use it for music.
Some of the verse that he wrote for use in his
songs is of uncommon quality—imaginative, distinguished in diction, and, above all, perfectly
suited to musical utterance. Of uncommon
quality, too, are some of the brief verses which
he used as mottos for certain of his later piano
pieces — as for the "Sea Pieces" and "New
England Idyls."

That his songs, as a whole, are comparable in
inherent artistic consequence with his sonatas,

or with such things as the "Woodland Sketches," the "Sea Pieces," and the "New England Idyls," I do not believe, although I readily grant the beauty and fascination of many passages, and of certain pages in which he is incontestably at the height of his powers.   Here, as in his writing for piano and for orchestra, one will find abundant evidence of his distinguishing traits — sensitiveness and fervour of imagination, a lovely and intimate sense of romance, whimsical and piquant humour, virility, passion, an unerring instinct for atmospheric suggestion. But there are times when, despite his avowed principles in the matter, he sacrifices truth of declamation to the presumed requirements of melodic design — when he seems to pay more heed to the unrelated effect of tonal contours than to the dramatic or emotional needs of his text. As an instance of his not infrequent indifference to justness of declamatory utterance, examine his setting of "in those brown eyes," at the bottom of the last page of "Confidence" (op. 47), and of the word "without" in the fourth bar of "Tyrant Love" (op. 60). I dwell upon this point, not in any spirit of captiousness, I need scarcely say, but because it exemplifies a fairly persistent characteristic of MacDowell's style as a song writer.

Of that other trait to which I have referred —

his not exceptional preoccupation with a purely musical plan at the expense of dramatic and emotional congruity — the attentive observer will not want for examples in almost any of Mac-Dowell's song-groups. As a single instance, I may allege the run in eighth-notes which encumbers the setting of the second syllable of the word "again," in the fourth bar of "Springtide" (op. 60). Such infelicities are difficult to account for in the work of a musician so exceedingly sensitive in matters of poetic fitness as he. It may be that his acute sense of dramatic and emotional values operated perfectly only when he was unhampered by the thought of the voice.

I have dwelt upon this point because it should be noted in any candid study of his traits as a song writer. Yet it is not a defect which weighs heavily against him when one considers the musical quality of his songs as a whole. Not, as a whole, equal to his piano music, they are admirable and deeply individual; and the best of them are not surpassed in any body of modern song-writing.

In almost all of his songs the voice is predominant over the piano part — although he is far, indeed, from writing mere accompaniments: the support which he gives the voice is consistently important, for he brings to bear upon it all his

rich resources of harmonic expression. But
though he makes the voice the paramount element, he uses it, in general, rather as a vehicle
for the unconscious exposition of a determined
lyricism than as an instrument of precise emotional utterance. When one thinks of how Hugo
Wolf, for example, or Debussy, would have
treated the phrase, "to wake again the bitter
joy of love," in "Fair Springtide," it will be felt,
I think, that MacDowell's setting leaves something to be desired on the score of emotional
verity, although the song, as a whole, is one of
the loveliest and most spontaneous he has written.
I do not mean to say that he does not often achieve
an ideal correspondence between the significance
of his text and the effect of his music; but when
he does — as in, for instance, that superb tragedy
in little, "The Sea,"* or in the still finer "Sunrise"† — one's impression is that it is the fortunate result of chance, rather than the outcome
of deliberate artistic purpose. It is in songs of
an untrammelled lyricism that his art finds its
chief opportunity. In such he is both delightful
and satisfying — in, for instance, the six flower
songs, "From an Old Garden"; in "Confidence"
and "In the Woods" (op. 47); in "The Swan

* No VII. of the "Eight Songs," op. 47.
† Op. 58, No. II.

Bent Low to the Lily," "A Maid Sings Light,"
and "Long Ago" (op. 56); and in the delectable
"To the Golden Rod," from his last song group
(op. 60). This is music of blithe and captivating
allurement, of grave or riant tenderness, of com-
pelling fascination; and in it, the word and the
tone are ideally mated. Yet even in others of
his songs in which they do not so invariably
correspond, one must acknowledge gladly the
beauty and freshness of the music itself: such
music as he has given us in "Constancy" (op.
58), in "As the Gloaming Shadows Creep"
(op. 56), in "Fair Springtide" — which represent
his ripest utterances as a song writer. If he is
not, in this particular form, quite at his happiest,
he is among the foremost of those who have kept
alive in the modern tradition the conception of
the song as a medium of lyric utterance no less
than of precise dramatic signification.

CHAPTER VIII

SUMMARY

To gain a true sense of MacDowell's place in American music it is necessary to remember that twenty-five years ago, when he sent from Germany, as the fruit of his apprenticeship there, the earliest outgivings of his talent, our native musical art was still little more than a pallid reproduction of European models. MacDowell did not at that time, of course, give positive evidence of the vitality and the rarity of his gifts; yet there was, even in his early music, — undeniably immature though it was, and modelled after easily recognised Teutonic masters, — a fresh and untrammelled impulse. A new note vibrated through it, a new and buoyant personality suffused it. Thenceforth music in America possessed an artistic figure of constantly increasing stature. MacDowell commanded, from the start, an original idiom, a manner of speech which has been recognised even by his detractors as entirely his own.

His style is as pungent and unmistakable as

Grieg's, and far less limited in its variety. Hearing certain melodic turns, certain harmonic formations, you recognise them at once as belonging to MacDowell, and to none other. This marked individuality of speech, apparent from the first, became constantly more salient and more vivid, and in the music which he gave forth at the height of his creative activity, — in, say, the "Sea Pieces" and the last two sonatas, — it is unmistakable and beyond dispute. This emphatically personal accent it was which, a score of years ago, set MacDowell in a place apart among native American music-makers. No one else was saying such charming and memorable things in so fresh and individual a way. We had then, as we have had since, composers who were entitled to respect by virtue of their expert and effective mastery of a familiar order of musical expression, — who spoke correctly a language acquired in the schools of Munich, Leipzig, and Berlin. But they had nothing to say that was both important and new. They had grace, they had dexterity, they had, in a measure, scholarship; but their art was obviously derivative, without originality of substance or a telling quality of style. It is not a needlessly harsh asseveration to say that, until MacDowell began to put forth his more individual works, our music had been palpably, almost frankly, dependent: an undisguised and naïve transplantation, made rather feeble and anæmic in the process, of European growths. The result was admirable, in its way, praiseworthy, in its way — and wholly negligible.

The music of MacDowell was, almost from the first, in a wholly different case. In its early phases it, too, was imitative, reflective. MacDowell returned to America, after a twelve years' apprenticeship to European influences, in 1888, bringing with him his symphonic poems, "Hamlet and Ophelia" and "Lancelot and Elaine," his unfinished "Lamia," his two orchestral paraphrases of scenes from the Song of Roland, two concertos, and numerous songs and piano pieces. Not greatly important music, this, measured beside that which he afterward put forth; but possessing an individual profile, a savour, a tang, which gave it an immediately recognised distinction. A new voice spoke out of it, a fresh and confident, an eloquent and forceful, voice. It betrayed Germanic influences: of that there was no question; yet it was strikingly rich in personal accent. Gradually his art came to find, through various forms, a constantly finer and weightier expression. For orchestra he wrote the "Indian" suite — music of superb vigour, fantastically and deeply imaginative, wholly personal in quality; for the piano he wrote four sonatas of heroic and passionate content — indisputable masterworks — and various shorter pieces, free in form and poetic in inspiration; and he wrote many songs, some of them quite flawless in their loveliness and their emotional veracity.

It will thus be seen why the potent and aromatic art of MacDowell impressed those who were able to feel its charm and estimate its value. It is mere justice to him, now that he has definitely passed beyond the reach of our praise, to say that he gave to the art of creative music in this country (I am thinking now only of music-makers of native birth) its single impressive and vital figure. His is the one name in our music which, for instance, one would venture to pair with that of Whitman in poetry.

An abundance of pregnant, beautiful, and novel ideas was his chief possession, and he fashioned them into musical designs with great skill and unflagging art. That he did not undertake adventures in all of the forms of music, has been said. There is no symphony in the list of his published works, no large choral composition. Yet he was far from being a miniaturist, — he was, in fact, anything but that. His four sonatas for the piano are planned upon truly heroic lines; they are large in scope and of epical sweep and breadth; and his "Indian" suite is the most impressive orchestral work composed by an American. He wrote two piano concertos, — early works, not of his best inspiration, — a large number of poetically descriptive smaller works, and almost half a hundred songs of frequent loveliness and character. The three symphonic poems, "Hamlet and Ophelia," "Lancelot and Elaine," and "Lamia"; the two "fragments," "The Saracens," and "The Lovely Aldâ," and the first orchestral suite, op. 42 — which he might have entitled "Sylvan" — complete the record of his output, save for some spirited but not very important part-songs for male voices. The list comprises sixty-two opus numbers and one hundred and eighty-six separate compositions, — not a remarkable accomplishment, in point of quantity, yet notable and rare in quality.

He suggested, at his best, no one save himself. He was one of the most individual writers who ever made music — as individual as Chopin, or Debussy, or Brahms, or Grieg. His manner of speech was utterly untrammelled, and wholly his own. Vitality — an abounding freshness, a perpetual youthfulness — was one of his prime

traits; nobility — nobility of style and impulse —
was another. The morning freshness, the welling
spontaneity of his music, even in moments of
exalted or passionate utterance, was continually
surprising: it was music not unworthy of the
golden ages of the world. Yet MacDowell was a
Celt, and his music is deeply Celtic — mercurial,
by turns dolorous and sportive, darkly tragical
and exquisitely blithe, and overflowing with the
unpredictable and inexplicable magic of the
Celtic imagination. He is unfailingly noble —
it is, in the end, the trait which most surely
signalises him. "To every man," wrote Maeter-
linck, "there come noble thoughts, thoughts that
pass across his heart like great white birds."
Such thoughts came often to MacDowell — they
seem always to be hovering not far from the particular territory to which his inspiration has led
him, even when he is most gayly inconsequent;
and in his finest and largest utterances, in the
sonatas, their majestic trend appears somehow to
have suggested the sweeping and splendid flight
of the musical idea. Not often subtle in impulse
or recondite in mood, his art has nothing of the
impalpability, the drifting, iridescent vapours of
Debussy, nothing of the impenetrable back-
grounds of Brahms. He would have smiled at
the dictum of Emerson: "a beauty not expli-

cable is dearer than a beauty of which we can see the end." He knew how to evoke a kind of beauty that was both aerial and enchanted; but it was a clarified and lucid beauty, even then: it was never dim or wavering. He would never, as I have said, have comprehended the art of such a writer as Debussy — he viewed the universe from a wholly different angle. Of the moderns, Wagner he worshipped, Tchaikovsky deeply moved him, Grieg he loved — Grieg, who was his artistic inferior in almost every respect. Yet none of these so seduced his imagination that his independence was overcome — he was always, throughout his maturity, himself; not arrogantly or insistently, but of necessity; he could not be otherwise.

What are the distinguishing traits, after all, of MacDowell's music? The answer is not easily given. His music is characterised by great buoyancy and freshness, by an abounding vitality, by a constantly juxtaposed tenderness and strength, by a pervading nobility of tone and feeling. It is charged with emotion, yet it is not brooding or hectic, and it is seldom intricate or recondite in its psychology. It is music curiously free from the fevers of sex. And here I do not wish to be misunderstood. This music is anything but androgynous. It is always virile, often passionate, and, in its intensest moments, full of force and vigour. But the sexual impulse which underlies it is singularly fine, strong, and controlled. The strange and burdened winds, the subtle delirium, the disorder of sense, that stir at times in the music of Wagner, Tchaikovsky, Debussy, are not to be found here. In Wagner, in certain songs by Debussy, one often feels, as Pater felt in William Morris's "King Arthur's Tomb," the tyranny of a moon which is "not tender and far-off, but close down — the sorcerer's moon, large and feverish," and the presence of a colouring that is "as of scarlet lilies"; and there is the suggestion of poison, with "a sudden bewildered sickening of life and all things." In the music of MacDowell there is no hint of these matters; there is rather the infinitely touching emotion of those rare beings who are in their interior lives both passionate and shy: they know desire and sorrow, supreme ardour and enamoured tenderness; but they do not know either the languor or the dementia of eroticism; they are haunted and swept by beauty, but they are not sickened or oppressed by it. Nor is their passion mystical and detached. MacDowell in his music is full-blooded, but he is never febrile: in this (though certainly in nothing else) he is like Brahms. The passion by which he is swayed is never, in its expression, ambiguous or exotic, his sensuousness is never luscious. It is difficult to think of a single passage from which that accent upon which I have dwelt — the accent of nobility, of a certain chivalry, a certain rare and spontaneous dignity — is absent. Yet he can be, withal, wonderfully tender and deeply impassioned, with a sharpness of emotion that is beyond denial. In such songs as "Deserted" (op. 9); "Menie" (op. 34); "The Robin Sings in the Apple Tree," "The West Wind Croons in the Cedar Trees" (op. 47); "The Swan Bent Low to the Lily," "As the Gloaming Shadows Creep" (op. 56); " Constancy" (op. 58); "Fair Springtide" (op. 60); in "Lancelot and Elaine"; in "Told at Sunset," from the "Woodland Sketches"; in "An Old Love Story," from "Fireside Tales": in this music the emotion is the distinctive emotion of sex; but it is the sexual emotion known to Burns rather than to Rossetti, to Schubert rather than to Wagner.

He had the rapt and transfiguring imagination, in the presence of nature, which is the special possession of the Celt. Yet he was more than a mere landscape painter. The human drama was for him a continually moving spectacle; he was most sensitively attuned to its tragedy and its comedy, — he was never more

potent, more influential, indeed, than in cele-
brating its events. He is at the summit of his
powers, for example, in the superb pageant of
heroic grief and equally heroic love which is
comprised within the three movements of the
"Keltic" sonata, and in the piercing sadness and
the transporting tenderness of the "Dirge" in
the "Indian" suite.

In its general aspect his later music is not
German, or French, or Italian — its spiritual antecedents are Northern, both Celtic and Scandinavian. MacDowell had not the Promethean
imagination, the magniloquent passion, that are
Strauss's; his art is far less elaborate and subtle
than that of such typical moderns as Debussy
and d'Indy. But it has an order of beauty that
is not theirs, an order of eloquence that is not
theirs, a kind of poetry whose secrets they do
not know; and there speaks through it and out
of it an individuality that is persuasive, lovable,
unique.

There is no need to attempt, at this juncture,
to speculate concerning his place among the
company of the greater dead; it is enough to
avow the conviction that he possessed genius of
a rare order, that he wrought nobly and valuably
for the art of the country which he loved.

LIST OF WORKS

COMPOSITIONS OF EDWARD MACDOWELL

Op. 9. *Two Old Songs,* for voice and piano (1894)*:
        1. Deserted
        2. Slumber Song
Op. 10. First *Modern Suite,* for piano (1883):
        Præladium — Presto — Andantino and
        Allegretto — Intermezzo — Rhapsody — Fugue
Op. 11. } *An Album of Five Songs,* for voice and piano
Op. 12. } (1883):
        1. My Love and I
        2. You Love me Not
        3. In the Skies
        4. Night-Song
        5. Bands of Roses
Op. 13. *Prelude and Fugue,* for piano (1883)
Op. 14. *Second Modern Suite,* for piano (1883):
        Præludium — Fugato — Rhapsody —
        Scherzino — March — Fantastic Dance
Op. 15. *First Concerto,* in A-minor, for piano and or-
        chestra (1885)
Op. 16. *Serenata,* for piano (1883)
Op. 17. *Two Fantastic Pieces,* for piano (1884):
        1. Legend
        2. Witches' Dance

*The publication dates given here are those of the original
editions.

Op. 18. *Two Compositions*, for piano (1884):
    1. Barcarolle
    2. Humoresque

Op. 19. *Forest Idyls*, for piano (1884):
    1. Forest Stillness
    2. Play of the Nymphs
    3. Revery
    4. Dance of the Dryads

Op. 20. *Three Poems*, for piano, four hands (1886):
    1. Night at Sea
    2. A Tale of the Knights
    3. Ballad

Op. 21. *Moon Pictures*, for piano, four hands (1886):
    1. The Hindoo Maiden
    2. Stork's Story
    3. In Tyrol
    4. The Swan
    5. Visit of the Bear

Op. 22. *Hamlet and Ophelia*, symphonic poem for orchestra (1885)

Op. 23. *Second Concerto*, in D-minor, for piano and orchestra (1890)

Op. 24. *Four Compositions*, for piano (1887):
    1. Humoresque
    2. March
    3. Cradle Song
    4. Czardas

Op. 25. *Lancelot and Elaine*, symphonic poem for orchestra (1888)

Op. 26. *From an Old Garden*, for voice and piano (1887):
    1. The Pansy
    2. The Myrtle
    3. The Clover

4. The Yellow Daisy
5. The Blue Bell
6. The Mignonette

Op. 27.   *Three Songs*, for male chorus (1890):
1. In the Starry Sky Above Us
2. Springtime
3. The Fisherboy

Op. 28.   *Six Idyls after Goethe*, for piano (1887):
1. In the Woods
2. Siesta
3. To the Moonlight
4. Silver Clouds
5. Flute Idyl
6. The Bluebell

Op. 29.   *Lamia*, symphonic poem for orchestra (1908)*

Op. 30.   *The Saracens; The Lovely Aldâ*, two fragments (after the Song of Roland), for orchestra (1891)

Op. 31.   *Six Poems after Heine*, for piano (1887):
1. From a Fisherman's Hut
2. Scotch Poem
3. From Long Ago
4. The Post Wagon
5. The Shepherd Boy
6. Monologue

Op. 32.   *Four Little Poems*, for piano (1888):
1. The Eagle
2. The Brook
3. Moonshine
4. Winter

Op. 33.   *Three Songs*, for voice and piano (1894):
1. Prayer

*Posthumous.

          2. Cradle Hymn

          3. Idyl

Op. 34. *Two Songs*, for voice and piano (1889):

          1. Menie

          2. My Jean

Op. 35. *Romance*, for violoncello and orchestra (1888)

Op. 36. *Étude de Concert*, in F-sharp, for piano (1889)

Op. 37. *Les Orientales*, for piano (1889):

          1. Clair de Lune

          2. Dans le Hamac

          3. Danse Andalouse

Op. 38. *Marionettes*, Eight Little Pieces, for piano (1888)*:

          1. Prologue

          2. Soubrette

          3. Lover

          4. Witch

          5. Clown

          6. Villain

          7. Sweetheart

          8. Epilogue

Op. 39. *Twelve Studies*, for piano (1890):

Book 1.
- Hunting Song
- Alla Tarantella
- Romance
- Arabesque
- In the Forest
- Dance of the Gnomes

* In their original form this set comprised only six pieces. MacDowell afterward revised them extensively, rearranged their order, and added the "Prologue" and "Epilogue." In this altered form they were published in 1901.

Book 2.
{ Idyl
Shadow Dance
Intermezzo
Melody
Scherzino
Hungarian

Op. 40. *Six Love Songs*, for voice and piano (1890):
1. Sweet, Blue-eyed Maid
2. Sweetheart, Tell Me
3. Thy Beaming Eyes
4. For Love's Sweet Sake
5. O Lovely Rose
6. I Ask but This

Op. 41. *Two Songs*, for male chorus (1890):
1. Cradle Song
2. Dance of the Gnomes

Op. 42. *First Suite*, for orchestra (1891–1893*):
1. In a Haunted Forest
2. Summer Idyl
3. In October
4. The Shepherdess' Song
5. Forest Spirits

Op. 43. *Two Northern Songs*, for mixed chorus (1891):
1. The Brook
2. Slumber Song

Op. 44. *Barcarolle*, for mixed chorus with four-hand piano accompaniment (1892)

* As originally published, in 1891, this suite comprised only the first, second, fourth, and fifth movements. The third, "In October," though composed at the same time as the others, and intended for inclusion in the suite, was not published until 1893, when it was issued as a "supplement" under the same opus number.

Op. 45. *Sonata Tragica*, for piano (1893)
Op. 46. *Twelve Virtuoso Studies*, for piano (1894):
  1. Novelette
  2. Moto Perpetuo
  3. Wild Chase
  4. Improvisation
  5. Elfin Dance
  6. Valse triste
  7. Burleske
  8. Bluette
  9. Träumerei
  10. March Wind
  11. Impromptu
  12. Polonaise
Op. 47. *Eight Songs*, for voice and piano (1893):
  1. The Robin Sings in the Apple Tree
  2. Midsummer Lullaby
  3. Folk Song
  4. Confidence
  5. The West Wind Croons in the Cedar Trees
  6. In the Woods
  7. The Sea
  8. Through the Meadow
Op. 48. *Second (Indian) Suite*, for orchestra (1897):
  1. Legend
  2. Love Song
  3. In War-time
  4. Dirge
  5. Village Festival
Op. 49. *Air and Rigaudon*, for piano (1894)
Op. 50. *Second Sonata (Eroica)*, for piano (1895)
Op. 51. *Woodland Sketches*, for piano (1896):
  1. To a Wild Rose
  2. Will'-o-the-Wisp

Op. 58. *Three Songs*, for voice and piano (1899):
    1. Constancy
    2. Sunrise
    3. Merry Maiden Spring

Op. 59. *Fourth Sonata* (*Keltic*), for piano (1901)

Op. 60. *Three Songs*, for voice and piano (1902):
    1. Tyrant Love
    2. Fair Springtide
    3. To the Golden Rod

Op. 61. *Fireside Tales*, for piano (1902):
    1. An Old Love Story
    2. Of Bre'r Rabbit
    3. From a German Forest
    4. Of Salamanders
    5. A Haunted House
    6. By Smouldering Embers

Op. 62. *New England Idyls*, for piano (1902):
    1. An Old Garden
    2. Midsummer
    3. Mid-winter
    4. With Sweet Lavender
    5. In Deep Woods
    6. Indian Idyl
    7. To an Old White Pine
    8. From Puritan Days
    9. From a Log Cabin
    10. The Joy of Autumn

WITHOUT OPUS NUMBER

Two Songs from the Thirteenth Century, for male chorus (1897):
    1. Winter Wraps his Grimmest Spell
    2. As the Gloaming Shadows Creep